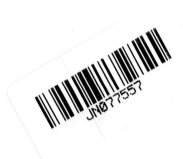

Simon Says

Basic English conversation for young adults

Simon Thollar

ACKNOWLEDGEMENT

Thanks to Bitmoji.com (Bitstrips Inc.) for generating characters. Also thanks to SomethingDrawn.com (p.17) and stockio.com for providing images (p.17). Thanks also to Nao for proofreading and translation checks.

DEDICATION

It is hoped that this text will invigorate English conversation among non-native speakers, and provide a springboard for further studies. With this in mind, I dedicate it to the more than 25,000 students that I have taught, and thank them for their courage.

The initial draft of this textbook was prepared on a MacBook Pro using Pages 09. Layout reformatted by Maruzen Planet.

Foreword

Simon Says is intended to be used as a textbook with young Japanese adults to help improve English language understanding and conversation skills. It is based on an earlier textbook, Speak Out, by the same author. The new book offers a combined graphic/ grammar model approach to improving conversation through incorporating cartoon-like characters demonstrating target sentences. It can be argued that too much writing in a book intimidates some students. With that in mind, a conscious attempt has been made to offer an alternative way to allow students to grasp basic English language patterns without being assaulted by complex grammatical structures.

Target vocabulary, expressions and idioms included in the book are expressed as simple graphic elements in a non-threatening manner. Key sentences are included in short light-hearted cartoon-like conversation between characters. Patterns and expressions are demonstrated through such banter. Over one hundred examples are in the text, and hopefully will allow students to gain a fundamental understanding of the meaning and usage.

Each chapter has been chosen for its relevance and is presented in a way that should prove interesting to the student. The level of difficulty has also been carefully chosen and each chapter builds upon new patterns learnt in the previous chapters. As the topics selected centre around every day situations, the dialogues, although simple, show the student how to competently and confidently communicate with an English speaker.

This book makes a conscious effort to use current conversational English in a number of realistic situations. Each chapter begins with a realistic dialogue (both in English and Japanese) where the main character, Yoko, finds herself in a number of everyday situations, demonstrating the necessary vocabulary and phrases. After the main dialogue, a number of shorter examples elucidating or developing the chapter's theme are presented. Following this, key points are demonstrated in a graphic context using cartoon-like representations of the main characters in the initial dialogue. This is in turn followed by a student exercise section. To facilitate understanding, Japanese explanations are used expediently. *Animated movies of the main dialogues will be made available online in the future.

Simon Says is intended to be a contemporary, conversational textbook. The language utilized has been consciously chosen for that purpose.

ST

Contents

*	*Foreword*	一言	iii
1	*How you doing?*	挨拶	1
2	*This is Paul.*	人と会う	11
3	*You doing anything?*	予定	21
4	*Let's go out!*	招待	31
5	*What can I get you?*	外食	41
6	*Got any tissues?*	持っている	51
7	*Crazy about Eric.*	好み	61
8	*Is John there?*	電話	71
9	*What's wrong with me?*	病気	81
10	*Never heard of it.*	経験	91
11	*In 2 weeks?*	過去未来	101
12	*I've been waiting.*	どのくらい	111
13	*Gotta go!*	提案	121
14	*Take care!*	別れ	131

"How you doing?"

QUICK START

挨拶	こんにちは。 元気ですか？ 君は？ はじめまして。 さようなら。	*Hi!* *How you doing?* *How/What about you?* *Nice to meet you.* *See ya.*	***Greetings***
自分	太郎です。 ... と呼んで ... の出身です	*I'm Taro/My name is Taro* *Call me ... .* *I'm from ... .*	***About you***
名前	下の名前 名字	*given name* *surname* or *family name*	***Names***
他	分かりました。 分かりません。 わかりますか？ 仕事は？	*I got it.* *I don't get it.* *You get it?* *What do you do?*	***Other***

You got it? (分かった？)

☺

- もう分かりましたか？
- チャレンジをやってみよう。
- *1f, 1g & 1h* (ページ*8~10*)にトライしよう。

- ***You got it?***
- ***Try the challenge section:***
- ***Exercises 1f, 1g, 1h (pages 8~10)***

☹

- まだ分かりませんか？
- まず、*1b, 1c, 1d & 1e*を読んで(ページ*2~7*)
- *1f, 1g & 1h* (ページ*8~10*)をトライしよう。

- ***You don't get it? Not sure?***
- ***Read Sections 1b, 1c, 1d & 1e (pages 2~7)***
- ***Then, try exercises 1f, 1g, 1h (pages 8~10)***

THE ENGLISH STORY

Greetings - John meets Yoko

1 Yoko: *Hello!*

2 John: *Hi! How' you doing?* [1]

3 Yoko: *Okay thanks.* [2] *How about you?* [3]

4 John: *Pretty good, thanks. By the way, what's your name?*

5 Yoko: *My name's Yoko. Yoko Sono. Just call me Yoko.* [4]

6 John: *I'm sorry. I didn't catch your surname. What's your surname again?*

7 Yoko: *It's Sono. What's your name?*

8 John: *I'm John Lemon.*

9 Yoko: *How do you spell your last name?* [5]

10 John: *L-E-M-O-N. Lemon. You got it?* [6]

11 Yoko: *I got it. Nice to meet you, John.* [7]

12 John: *It's good to meet you too, Yoko. Are you from Hong Kong?*

13 Yoko: *No. I'm from Osaka, Japan. Where are you from?* [8]

14 John: *I'm from Sydney, Australia.*

15 Yoko: *Oh, really? A friend of mine lives in Sydney.*

16 John: *It's a small world, isn't it.*

17 Yoko: *Yeah. What do you do,* [9] *John?*

18 John: *I'm a teacher. What about you, Yoko?*

19 Yoko: *Me? I'm a nurse. Gee, it's already 5. I have to go. I start work at 5:30.*

20 John: *Yeah. I have to go too. I've got to meet my friend, Paul.*

21 Yoko: *It was great meeting you. See you later.*

22 John: *Okay. See ya around,* [10] *Yoko.*

THE JAPANESE STORY

1C
挨拶

挨拶 - ジョンはヨーコと出会います。

1 ヨーコ: こんにちは!

2 ジョン: やあ! 元気?[1]

3 ヨーコ: ええ、元気だよ。[2] あなたは?[3]

4 ジョン: 僕も調子いいよ。ところで君の名前は?

5 ヨーコ: ヨーコです。曽野ヨーコです。ヨーコって呼んで。[4]

6 ジョン: すみませんが、名字をちょっと聞き取れなかった。名字、なんだって?

7 ヨーコ: 曽野です。あなたの名前は?

8 ジョン: ジョン レモンだよ。

9 ヨーコ: 名字[5]のスペルは?

10 ジョン: L-E-M-O-N。レモン。分かった?[6]

11 ヨーコ: 分かったわ。はじめまして、ジョン。[7]

12 ジョン: はじめまして、ヨーコさん。香港の出身かな?

13 ヨーコ: ちがいます。日本の大阪の生まれです。どこの出身ですか?[8]

14 ジョン: オーストラリアのシドニーの出身だよ。

15 ヨーコ: そうですか?友達がシドニーに住んでいますが。

16 ジョン: 世界は狭いね。

17 ヨーコ: そうですね。ジョンは何の仕事をしているの?[9]

18 ジョン: 学校の先生だよ。ヨーコさんは?

19 ヨーコ: 私ですか?看護師です。もう5時ですね。行かないと。5時半から仕事があります。

20 ジョン: そうだね。僕も行かないと。ポールという友達と会う約束があるんだ。

21 ヨーコ: 会えてよかった。さようなら。

22 ジョン: うん。またね、[10] ヨーコさん。

1d
挨拶

EXAMPLES

A: How you going, Paul?
B: I'm pretty good. How about you?
A: Not bad thanks.

* * *

A: How's everything, Ringo?
B: Okay thanks. What about you?
A: Fairly good.

* * *

A: Hey Jude, how's it going?
B: Great! How about you?
A: I'm fine thanks, Paul.

* * *

A: Where are you from?
B: I'm from England. How 'bout you?
A: I'm from Sapporo, Japan.

* * *

A: What do you do, Michael?
B: I'm a singer. What about you, Tom?
A: I'm only an actor.

* * *

A: My given name's Kazuya, and my family name is Sato. Please call me Kazu.
B: Nice to meet you, Kazu.

* * *

A: I don't get it. What does $H_2$0 mean?
B: OK. $H_2$0 means water! You got it?
A: Yeah. Now I follow you!

A: ポール、元気？
B: すごく元気。君は？
A: まぁ、元気だね。

* * *

A: リンゴ、元気かい？
B: うん、元気。君は？
A: 元気だよ。

* * *

A: ねえ、ジュード。どうだい？
B: うん、いい感じだね。君は？
A: うん、元気だよ、ポール。

* * *

A: どこの出身ですか？
B: 僕はイギリスの出身です。君は？
A: 僕は日本の札幌の出身です。

* * *

A: マイケル、君は仕事は何してるの？
B: 僕は歌手よ。トム、君は？
A: 僕はただの俳優だよ。

* * *

A: おれの名前はカズヤ、名字はサトウです。 カズと呼んで。
B: はじめまして、カズさん。

* * *

A: 分からない！ $H_2$0ってどういう意味？
B: いいよ。$H_2$0は水のことだよ。分かった？
A: うん。今、分かった。

LEARN THESE SENTENCES

1　元気？　How you doing?

Hi.
How you doing?

Look at the diagram. Do you understand? They are all the same.

標準日本語	標準英語	会話的
お元気ですか？ →	How are you? →	*How (are) you doing?* *How (are) you going?* *How's it going?* *How's everything?*

2　元気です。 Okay thanks.

Hi.
How's everything?
Pretty good.
Good thanks.
Not bad.
I'm OK.
Fairly good.
Fine.
OK thanks.
I'm great!
Not so good.

Look at the diagram. There are many answers!

標準日本語	標準英語	会話的
元気ですよ。 →	I'm fine thanks. →	*I'm good.* *Pretty good* *Not bad.* *I'm fairly good.* *OK thanks.* 等

3　あなたは？　How about you?

Hi.
How you going?
I'm great!
How 'bout you?
Fine thanks.

Look at the diagram. Don't say, "And you?".

And youより How 'bout youの方がかっこいいよ。

標準日本語	標準英語	会話的
君は？ →	How about you? What about you? →	*How 'bout you?* *What about you?*

4　ヨーコって呼んで。　Just call me Yoko.

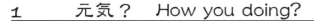

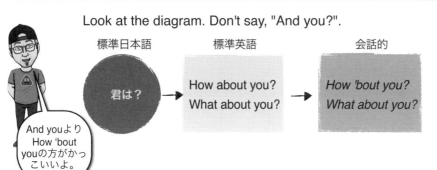

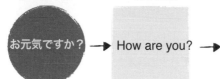

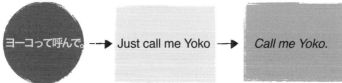

Call me Yoko.
Please call me John.

Look at the diagram. Do you understand?

標準日本語	標準英語	会話的
ヨーコって呼んで。 →	Just call me Yoko →	*Call me Yoko.*

LEARN THESE SENTENCES

5 名字・名前 last name/first name

Look at the diagram. Do you understand?

標準日本語	標準英語	会話的
名字・姓 →	last name →	*family name* *surname*
名前 →	first name →	*given name*

My first name is Yoko.
My given name's John.

My family name is Lemon.
My surname's Sono.

6 分かった？ You got it?

Look at the diagram. Do you understand?

	標準日本語	標準英語	会話的
?	分かりましたか？ →	Do you understand? →	*(Do) you get it?* *(Do) you follow me?* *(Are) you with me?*
+	分かりました。 →	I understand. →	*I get it. (I got it)* *I follow you.* *I'm with you.*
–	分かりません。 →	I don't understand. →	*I don't get it.* *I don't follow you.* *I'm not with you.*

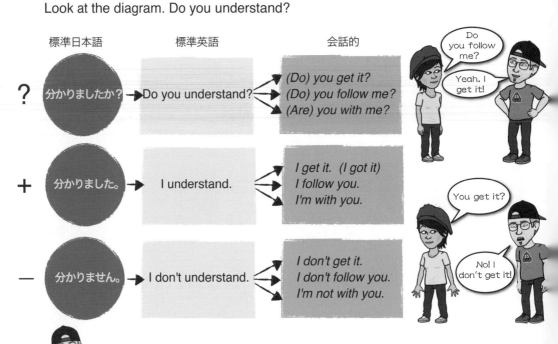

Do you follow me?
Yeah. I get it!

You get it?
No! I don't get it!

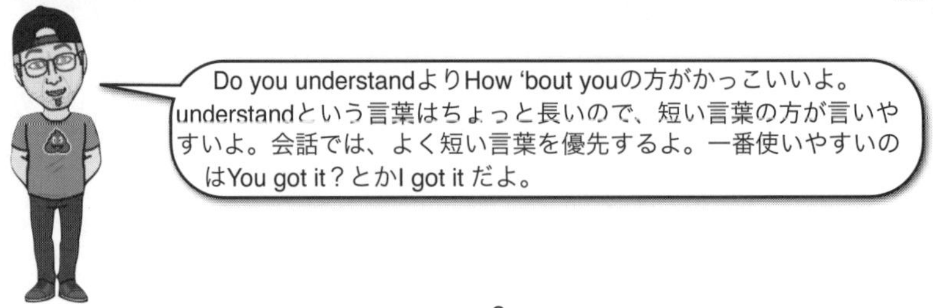
Do you understandよりHow 'bout youの方がかっこいいよ。understandという言葉はちょっと長いので、短い言葉の方が言いやすいよ。会話では、よく短い言葉を優先するよ。一番使いやすいのはYou got it？とかI got itだよ。

LEARN THESE SENTENCES

7　はじめまして　Nice to meet you.

Look at the diagram. Do you understand?

もっと丁寧に話しかったら、How do you do? を使おう。

標準日本語	標準英語	会話的
はじめまして。	(I'm) pleased to meet you. (I'm) glad to meet you. (I'm) happy to meet you. (It's) nice to meet you. (It's) good to meet you.	*Pleased to meet you.* *Glad to meet you.* *Happy to meet you.* *Nice to meet you.* *Good to meet you.*

Hi. Glad to meet you.
Nice to meet you.

8　どこの出身ですか？　Where are you from?

Look at the diagram. Do you understand?

標準日本語	標準英語	会話的
どこの出身ですか？	Where are you from?	*Where (are) you from?*

Hi. Where you from?
Tokyo. How bout you?
Me? I'm from Sydney.

9　仕事は何ですか？　What do you do?

Look at the diagram. Do you understand?

標準日本語	標準英語	会話的
お仕事は何ですか？	What do you do for a living?	*What do you do?*

What do you do?
I'm a dancer!

10　またね。　See ya around

Look at the diagram. Do you understand?

See ya!
OK. Later!

標準日本語	標準英語	会話的
さようなら	See you. See you around. See you later. Catch you later. Goodbye. Bye bye. Bye.	*See ya.* *See ya 'round.* *See ya later.* *Later.* *Catch ya later.* *G'bye.* *B'bye.* *Bye.*

挨拶に you を使わなでね。yaを使ってね。

CHALLENGE STAGE

Challenge 1. *Fill in the blanks from the list.*

1	Simon:	Hello.
2	Garfunkel:	Hi! 元気ですか。
3	Simon:	Good thanks. 君は？
4	Garfunkel:	元気だよ。 By the way, what's your name?
5	Simon:	My name's Phil. Phil Simon. フィルって呼んで下さい。
6	Garfunkel:	I'm sorry, Phil. 名字を聞き取れなかった。 What's your surname again?
7	Simon:	It's Simon. 名前は何というの？
8	Garfunkel:	My name's Bart. Bart Garfunkel.
9	Simon:	How do you spell your last name, Bart?
10	Garfunkel:	It's G-A-R-F-U-N-K-E-L. Garfunkel. Okay?
11	Simon:	Okay. I follow you. はじめまして、バート。
12	Garfunkel:	よろしくお願いします、フィル。 Are you from England?
13	Simon:	No. I'm from the States. How about you?
14	Garfunkel:	I'm from the States, too.
15	Simon:	Really! バートの仕事は何ですか？
16	Garfunkel:	I'm a singer. フィルは？
17	Simon:	Me? I'm a song-writer.
18	Garfunkel:	It's a small world, isn't it? Gee, it's already 7. I gotta go.
19	Simon:	Yeah. Me too. 会えた良かったよ、バート。 See you later.
20	Garfunkel:	Sure. またねフィル。

Choose the best sentence for the blanks:

a) How about you?
b) Please call me Phil.
c) What's your name?
d) It's good to meet you too, Phil.
e) What about you, Phil?
f) It was great meeting you, Bart.
g) See you 'round, Phil.
h) How you doing?
i) Not bad, thanks.
j) I didn't catch your surname.
k) Nice to meet you, Bart.
l) What do you do, Bart?

CHALLENGE STAGE

Challenge 2. *Circle the correct answer.*

1. Which expression does NOT mean *How are you?*
   - (a) How you going?
   - (b) How's everything?
   - (c) How you doing?
   - (d) What you doing?

2. Which expression is NOT a good answer for *How's it going?*
   - (a) Pretty good.
   - (b) OK thanks.
   - (c) I'm god, thank you.
   - (d) Not bad.

3. Which expression means *And you?*
   - (a) How about you?
   - (b) What about yours?
   - (c) How do you do?
   - (d) What do you do?

4. When you meet someone for the first time, which expression is NOT a good thing to say?
   - (a) Nice to meet you.
   - (b) Glad to meet you.
   - (c) Pleased to meet you.
   - (d) Happy to eat you.

5. Which expression means *last name*?
   - (a) Given name
   - (b) Middle name
   - (c) Folk name
   - (d) Surname

6. Which expression means *first name*?
   - (a) Given name
   - (b) Family name
   - (c) Friendly name
   - (d) Surname

7. Which expression is NOT similar to *Goodbye*?
   - (a) See you later.
   - (b) Catch you later.
   - (c) See you around.
   - (d) See you yesterday.

8. If you don't understand somebody, which expression is NOT a good reply?
   - (a) I don't follow you.
   - (b) I didn't catch what you said.
   - (c) I don't know your words.
   - (d) I don't get it.

9. If you want someone to use you *first name (e.g. John)*, what do you say?
   - (a) Say me John.
   - (b) Call me John.
   - (c) Speak me John.
   - (d) Talk me John.

10. If you want to ask somebody about *their job*, what do you say?
    - (a) What do you work?
    - (b) How do you do?
    - (c) How is your work?
    - (d) What do you do?

CHALLENGE STAGE

Challenge 3. *Did you read the English story?*
Let's check!

1. What is Yoko's surname?
   - *(i) Her surname is Yoko.*
   - *(ii) Her surname is Sono.*
   - *(iii) Her surname is Lemon.*
   - *(iv) Her surname is John.*

2. What is John's family name?
   - *(i) His family name is Yoko.*
   - *(ii) His family name is Sono.*
   - *(iii) His family name is Lemon.*
   - *(iv) His family name is John.*

3. What does Yoko do?
   - *(i) She is a nurse.*
   - *(ii) She is a teacher.*
   - *(iii) She is studying English.*
   - *(iv) She is talking.*

4. What does John do?
   - *(i) He is a nurse.*
   - *(ii) He is a teacher.*
   - *(iii) He is meeting his friends.*
   - *(iv) He is speaking.*

5. Where is Yoko from?
   - *(i) She's from Tokyo.*
   - *(ii) She's from Osaka.*
   - *(iii) She's from Sydney.*
   - *(iv) She's from Hong Kong.*

6. Where is John from?
   - *(i) He's from Sydney.*
   - *(ii) He's from Tokyo.*
   - *(iii) He's from Hong Kong.*
   - *(iv) He's from Japan.*

7. Where does Yoko's friend live?
   - *(i) Her friend lives in Sydney.*
   - *(ii) Her friend lives in Osaka.*
   - *(iii) Her friend lives in Hong Kong.*
   - *(iv) Her friend lives in Tokyo.*

8. What time does Yoko start work?
   - *(i) She starts work at 5:30.*
   - *(ii) She starts work at 5:00.*
   - *(iii) She starts work at 8:00.*
   - *(iv) She starts work at 6:00.*

9. Who does John have to meet?
   - *(i) He has to meet Yoko.*
   - *(ii) He has to meet his friend Paul.*
   - *(iii) He has to meet his friend in Sydney.*
   - *(iv) He has to meet his teacher.*

10. In the story, what time is it?
    - *(i) It's noon.*
    - *(ii) It's 5:30.*
    - *(iii) It's 5:00.*
    - *(iv) It's late.*

2a
人と会う

"This is Paul."

QUICK START

挨拶		（私のことを）覚えてる？	*Remember me?*	**Greetings**
		元気でしたか。	*How have you been?*	
		元気だったかい。	*How've you been?*	
	Ch1	君は？	*How/What about you?*	
	Ch1	はじめまして。	*Nice to meet you.*	
楽しい		日本を楽しんでいますか？	*Are you enjoying Japan?*	**Fun!**
		楽しんでいますか？	*Are you enjoying yourself?*	
		楽しいです。	*I'm having a good time.*	
紹介		こちらはジョンです。	*This is John.*	**Introducing**
		あの人は誰ですか？	*Who's that?*	
		こっちへ来て。	*Come (over) here.*	
誰？		あの男性は誰ですか？	*Who's that guy?*	**Who?**
		あの女性は誰ですか？	*Who's that girl?*	
		あのハゲは誰ですか？	*Who's the bald guy?*	
		帽子をかぶっている人は誰？	*Who's the guy with the hat?*	

You got it? (分かった？)

☺ ☹

・もう分かりましたか？
・チャレンジをやってみよう。
・*2f, 2g & 2h* (ページ*18~20*)にトライしよう。

・*You got it?*
・*Try the challenge section:*
・*Exercises 2f, 2g, 2h (pages 18~20)*

・まだ分かりませんか？
・まず、*2b, 2c, 2d & 2e*を読んで(ページ*12~17*)
・*2f, 2g & 2h* (ページ*18~20*)にトライしよう。

・*You don't get it? Not sure?*
・*Read Sections 2b, 2c, 2d & 2e (pages 12~17)*
・*Then, try exercises 2f, 2g, 2h (pages 18~20)*

2b
人と会う

THE ENGLISH STORY

Meeting People - Yoko meets some of John's friends

1 John: *Yoko! Remember me?*[1] *We met last week!*

2 Yoko: *Sure. I remember you! You're John, right?*

3 John: *Yeah. Come over here*[2] *and meet my friends.*

4 Yoko: *Okay.*

5 John: *Anyway Yoko, how have you been?*[3]

6 Yoko: *I've been pretty good. What about you?*

7 John: *Great, thanks. Are you enjoying Australia?*[4]

8 Yoko: *Sure. I'm having a really good time, thanks.*

9 John: *Good. Yoko, this is my friend, Paul.*[5] *He's from England and he's a musician. Paul, this is Yoko. She's from Osaka, Japan and she's a nurse.*

10 Paul: *It's nice to meet you, Yoko.*

11 Yoko: *Nice to meet you too, Paul.*

12 John: *Some of my other friends are having a barbecue over there.*

13 Yoko: *I can see them. Who's that fat guy?*[6]

14 John: *Yoko! Don't say fat. Say large!*

15 Yoko: *Sorry. Who's the large guy?*

16 John: *That's Ringo. He's talking to Mic.*

17 Yoko: *Who's that blonde girl?*

18 John: *That's Paul's girlfriend, Linda. She's taking a photo of Keith.*

19 Yoko: *Who's the guy with the long hair?*[7]

20 John: *That's George. He's drinking with his friends from India.*

21 Yoko: *Who's the bald guy?*

22 John: *That's Alcindo. He's playing soccer with Gary.*

23 Yoko: *You sure have a lot of friends, John.*

THE JAPANESE STORY

2c
人と会う

人と会う - ヨーコはジョンの友達と会います。

1 ジョン: ヨーコ！ 僕を覚えてる？[1] 先週会ったよね。

2 ヨーコ: もちろん覚えてるわよ！ ジョンでしょ？

3 ジョン: こっちに来て[2] 僕の友達に会わないかい？

4 ヨーコ: いいわよ。

5 ジョン: それはともかく、ヨーコ、元気だったかい？[3]

6 ヨーコ: とても元気だったわ。ジョンは？

7 ジョン: 僕も元気さ。（ありがとう。）オーストラリアを楽しんでるかい？[4]

8 ヨーコ: ええ、ほんとうに楽しいわ。（ありがとう。）

9 ジョン: よかった。ヨーコ、こちらは友達のポールだよ。[5] イギリス出身でミュージシャンなんだ。ポール、こちらはヨーコ。日本の大阪出身で看護師なんだ。

10 ポール: どうぞよろしく、ヨーコ。

11 ヨーコ: どうぞよろしくね、ポール。

12 ジョン: 他の友達が何人かあっちでバーベキューをしてるんだ。

13 ヨーコ: ええ、見えるわ。あのデブは誰？[6]

14 ジョン: ヨーコ！ 「デブ」って言っちゃだめだよ。「大きい」って言わなくちゃ。

15 ヨーコ: ごめんなさい。あの大きい人は誰？

16 ジョン: あれはリンゴだよ。ミックと話してるんだ。

17 ヨーコ: あの金髪の女の子は？

18 ジョン: ポールのガールフレンド、リンダだ。キースの写真を撮っているところだね。

19 ヨーコ: あの長髪（ロン毛）の人は？[7]

20 ジョン: あれはジョージ。インドから来てる友達と飲んでいるんだね。

21 ヨーコ: あの禿げた人は誰？

22 ジョン: あれはアルシンドだね。ギャリーとサッカーをしているね。

23 ヨーコ: ジョン、あなたはほんとうに友達が多いのね。

A: How have you been?
B: Not bad. How about you?
A: Good thanks.

* * *

A: How've you been?
B: Fine thanks. What about you?
A: Pretty good.

* * *

A: Bob, this is Cate. Cate, this is Bob.
B: Pleased to meet you, Cate.
C: Nice to meet you too, Bob.

* * *

A: Bill, this is Ted. Ted, Bill.
T: How' you doing Bill.
B: Good. Great to know you, Ted.

* * *

A: Are you having a good time?
B: Sure. How about you?
A: Yeah. I'm enjoying myself.

* * *

A: Who's the tall bald guy?
B: That's Jason.

* * *

A: Who's the guy with the nice body?
B: That's Dwayne.

* * *

A: Who's that girl with the camera?
B: That's Annie.

A: 元気でしたか？
B: うん、まあまあ。君は？
A: まあね。

* * *

A: 元気でしたか？
B: 元気でしたよ。君は？
A: とても元気だよ。

* * *

A: ボブ、こちらはケイト。ケイト、ボブ。
B: ケイトさんどうぞよろしく。
C: ボブ、はじめまして。

* * *

A: ビル、こちらはテッド。テッド、ビル。
T: ビル、元気？
B: テッド、はじめまして。

* * *

A: 楽しい？
B: うん、楽しいよ。君は？
A: 楽しいです。

* * *

A: 背の高い禿げてる人は誰？
B: あれはジェイソンだよ。

* * *

A: いい体してる男は誰ですか？
B: あれはドウェインです。

* * *

A: カメラを持ってる女性は誰？
B: 彼女はアニーだよ。

LEARN THESE SENTENCES

1 覚えてる？ Remember me?

Look at the diagram. Do you understand?

標準日本語	標準英語	会話的
覚えてる？	Do you remember me?	*Remember me?*

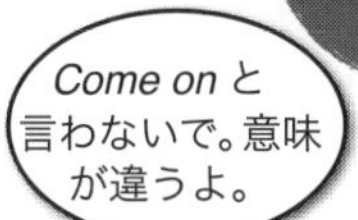

2 こっちに来て。 Come over here.

Look at the diagram. There are 2 good expressions!

標準日本語	標準英語	会話的
こっちに来て。	Please come here.	*Come over here.* *Come here.* *(C'mere!)*

3 元気でしたか？ How have you been?

Look at the diagram. If we meet someone after a long time, we often say, "How have you been?" or "How've you been?"

標準日本語	標準英語	会話的
元気でしたか？	How have you been?	*How've you been?* *How ya been?*

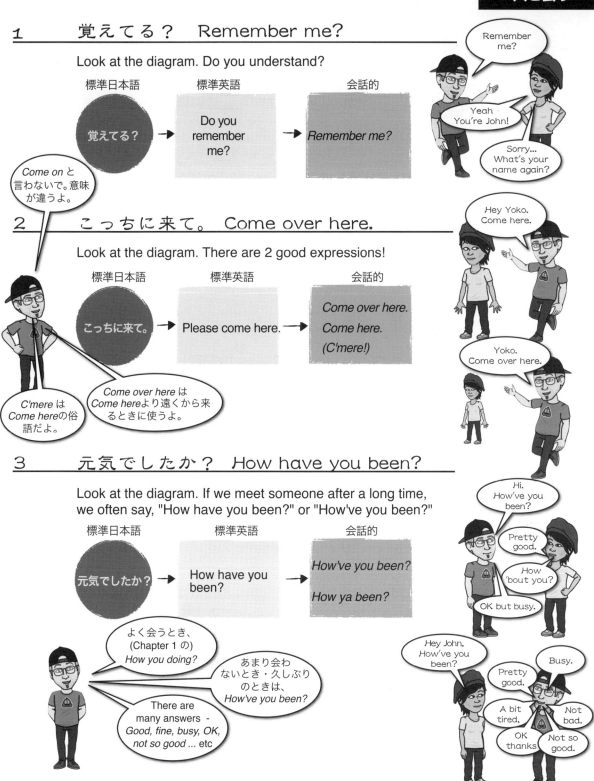

LEARN THESE SENTENCES

4 楽しんでいますか。 Are you enjoying yourself?

Look at the diagram. Do you understand?

Are you enjoying yourself?
Yes, I am.

標準日本語	標準英語	会話的
楽しんでいますか？ →	Are you enjoying yourself? →	*(Are) you enjoying yourself?* *Enjoying yourself?* *(Are) you having a good time?*

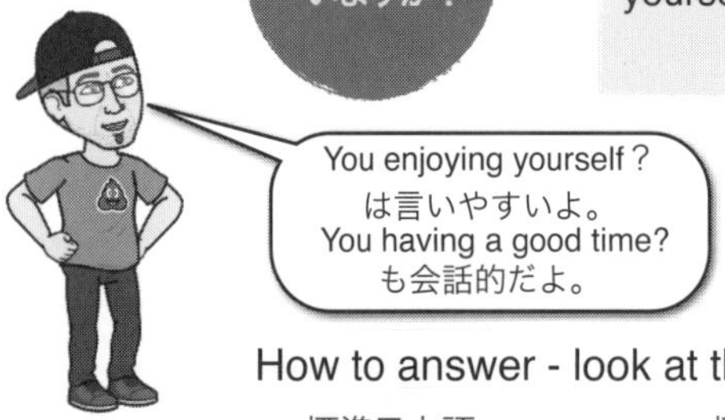
You enjoying yourself？
は言いやすいよ。
You having a good time?
も会話的だよ。

How to answer - look at the diagram. Do you understand?

You enjoying yourself?
Yeah, I'm enjoying the party.

	標準日本語	標準英語	会話的
☺	楽しいです。 →	Yes, I'm enjoying myself. →	*Yes, I'm enjoying myself.* *Yeah, I'm enjoying the party.*
☺	楽しいです。 →	Yes, I'm having a good time. →	*Yes, I'm having a good time.* *Yeah, I'm having a great time.*

You having a good time?
I'm having a great time!

Party だったら、I'm enjoying the party
とも言えるよ。同じように、I'm enjoying
the movie とも言えるよ。

	標準日本語	標準英語	会話的
☹	楽しくありません。 →	No, I'm not enjoying myself. →	*No, I'm not enjoying myself.* *No, I'm not enjoying the party.*
☹	楽しくありません →	No, I'm not having a good time. →	*No, I'm having a bad time.* *Nah, I'm having a terrible time.*

Are you enjoying yourself?
I'm not enjoying myself!

You having a nice time?
I'm having a really bad time!

LEARN THESE SENTENCES

5　ヨーコ、こちらはポールです。 Yoko, this is Paul.

Hi. Glad to meet you.
Nice to meet you.

Look at the diagram. Do you understand?

標準日本語	標準英語	会話的
A, こちらは B	A, this is B. Paul, this is Yoko. Mr Smith, this is Ms Jones.	*same*

MrとMsを使った方が丁寧だよ。使うとしたら、下の名前ではなくて、名字に付けてね。e.g. Mr Sasaki, Mr Taro Sasakiは良いけどが Mr Taroはちょっと不自然だよ。

標準日本語	標準英語	会話的
はじめまして	It's nice to meet you. (etc) How do you do? Hello, how are you?	*Good to meet you.* *Great to meet you.* *How'd you do?* *Hi, how you doing?*

How do you do?は、丁寧な言い方だよ。

meetの変わりにknowを使う人もいるよ。

Hi. Where you from?
Tokyo, How bout you?
Me? I'm from Sydney.

6　あの人は誰ですか？　Who's that guy?

Look at the diagram. Do you understand?

標準日本語	標準英語	会話的
あの人は誰ですか？	Who is he/she? Who is he? Who is she?	*Who's that?* *Who's that guy?* *Who's that lady?* *Who's that tall lady?*

Who is he/she よりWho's thatの方が会話的だよ。

Who's that guy?
That's Santa.

7　あの長髪（ロン毛）の人は？　Who's that guy with the..?

Look at the diagram. Do you understand?

標準日本語	標準英語	会話的
あの長髪の人は誰ですか？	Who is the person who has long hair? Who is the lady who is wearing a red hat? Who is the man who is walking the big dog?	*Who's the guy **with** the long hair?* *Who's that lady **with** the red hat?* *Who's that guy **with** the big dog?*

Who's <u>the</u> guy...かWho's <u>that</u> guy...か、どちらでもいいよ。

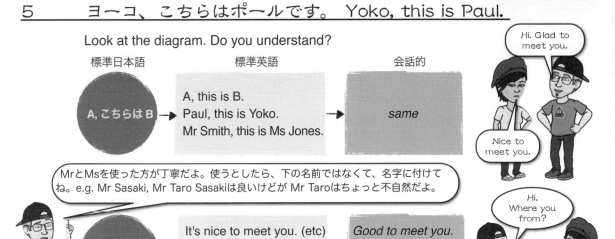

Who's that guy with the grey beard?
That's Santa.

2f
人と会う

CHALLENGE STAGE

Challenge 1. *Fill in the blanks from the list.*

1	Tom:	Hey, Jerry. 覚えてる？ We met on Friday.
2	Jerry:	もちろん！ I remember you. トムだね。
3	Tom:	That's right. Come over here and meet one of my friends.
4	Jerry:	Okay.
5	Tom:	Anyway, Jerry, 元気でしたか？
6	Jerry:	とても元気でしたよ。ありがとう。 What about you?
7	Tom:	Really good thanks. Are you enjoying America?
8	Jerry:	Sure! とても楽しいです。
9	Tom:	Great. Jerry, this is my friend Frankie. Frankie, this is Jerry.
10	Frankie:	Hi. Nice to meet you, Jerry.
11	Jerry:	どうぞよろしく、フランキー。
12	Tom:	Some of my other friends are playing basketball over there.
13	Jerry:	I can see them. Who's the skinny guy?
14	Tom:	ほら、skinnyと言わないで！ Say slim!
15	Jerry:	Sorry. Who's the slim guy?
16	Tom:	That's George. He's passing the ball to Donald.
17	Jerry:	あの背の高い人は誰ですか？
18	Tom:	The tall guy is Michael. He's throwing the ball to Magic.
19	Jerry:	トムは友達がいっぱいいるね。

Choose the best sentence for the blanks:

a) Sure!
b) Don't say 'skinny'!
c) I'm having a really good time.
d) How have you been?
e) Nice to meet you too, Frankie.
f) Who's the tall guy?
g) Remember me?
h) You sure have a lot of friends, Tom!
i) You're Tom, right?
j) I've been pretty good, thanks.

CHALLENGE STAGE

Challenge 2. *Circle the correct answer.*

1. The answer is *Yeah, you're Peter, right?* What's the question?
   (a) Are you remembering me? (b) Remember me?
   (c) Do you forget me? (d) What's your name?

2. You see your friend. You say 「こっちに来て！」. What do you say in English?
   (a) Come on! (b) Come to!
   (c) Come by! (d) Come here!

3. The answer is *I've been good.* What is the question?
   (a) How are you? (b) How have you been?
   (c) How have you doing? (d) How are you doing?

4. Which expression means *Are you enjoying yourself?*
   (a) Are you having a good time? (b) Are you happy?
   (c) Are you enjoy time? (d) Are you joyful time?

5. Introduction: *Mr A, this is Mr B. Mr B, this is Mr A.* What does Mr. A say?
   (a) Nice to eat you. (b) How do you do?
   (c) Good evening, sir. (d) Gee, you're ugly!

6. Introduction: *Ann, this is Ben. Ben, this is Ann.* What does Ann say?
   (a) How've you been? (b) Good to talk to you.
   (c) Happy we are meeting. (d) Nice to meet you.

7. *Ringo, this is George. George, Ringo.* Which expression is NOT GOOD for Ringo to say?
   (a) Hi, how you doing? (b) I'm very nice meeting you.
   (c) Glad to meet you. (d) How do you do?

8. Choose the best answer. Peter is introducing Mary to Paul.
   Paul, this is Mary. She's from England and [. . . . . .].
   (a) She is Mary. (b) She is fat.
   (c) She is fine, thanks. (d) She is a model.

9. Which expression is best?
   (a) Who's the guy has long hair? (b) Who's the guy have long hair?
   (c) Who's the guy on long hair? (d) Who's the guy with the long hair?

10. The question is *Who's the fat guy?* A good answer is:
    (a) Don't say fat! Say big. (b) Don't say big! Say fat.
    (c) Don't say large! Say fat. (d) That's my brother!

CHALLENGE STAGE

Challenge 3. Did you read the English story?
Let's check!

1. Is Yoko enjoying Australia?
   - *(i) She's having a bad time.*
   - *(ii) She's having a really good time.*
   - *(iii) She isn't having a good time.*
   - *(iv) She isn't enjoying Australia.*

2. What is the name of John's friend?
   - *(i) His name is Paul.*
   - *(ii) His name is Yoko.*
   - *(iii) His name is Alcindo.*
   - *(iv) His name is John.*

3. Where is he from?
   - *(i) He is from Australia.*
   - *(ii) He is from Osaka.*
   - *(iii) He is from India.*
   - *(iv) He is from England.*

4. What does he do?
   - *(i) He is a nurse.*
   - *(ii) He is a teacher.*
   - *(iii) He is a musician.*
   - *(iv) He is speaking.*

5. What are John's other friends doing?
   - *(i) They are playing baseball.*
   - *(ii) They are studying.*
   - *(iii) They are talking to John.*
   - *(iv) They are having a barbecue (bbq).*

6. Who's the large guy?
   - *(i) The large guy is Ringo.*
   - *(ii) The large guy is Paul.*
   - *(iii) The large guy is George.*
   - *(iv) The large guy is Alcindo.*

7. Who is he talking to?
   - *(i) He's talking to Keith.*
   - *(ii) He's talking to Mic.*
   - *(iii) He's talking to George.*
   - *(iv) He's talking to John.*

8. What is Paul's girlfriend's name?
   - *(i) Her name is Paul.*
   - *(ii) Her name is Yoko.*
   - *(iii) Her name is Betty.*
   - *(iv) Her name is Linda.*

9. What is she doing?
   - *(i) She's taking a photo of Keith.*
   - *(ii) She's playing soccer.*
   - *(iii) She's talking to Yoko.*
   - *(iv) She's sleeping.*

10. Who's the guy with the long hair?
    - *(i)* The guy with the long hair is George.
    - *(ii)* The guy with the long hair is Gary.
    - *(iii)* The guy with the long hair is Keith.
    - *(iv)* The guy with the long hair is Paul.

"You doing anything?"

3a
予定

ヨーコ、今晩
どうするの？
テレビ見る。
ジョンは？
ボーリング
しに行く。

Yoko,
What are you
doing
tonight?
I'm
watching TV.
How 'bout
you?
I'm
going bowling.

QUICK START

Y/N	うん、はい いやあ、ううん、いいえ	*Yeah, Yep, Uh-huh* *Nah, Nope, Uh-uh*	**Yes/No**
未来	今晩どうするの？／何するの？ どうするの？／何するの？ どうする？／何するの？	*What are you doing tonight?* *What are you going to do?* *What (are) you gonna do?*	**Future**
しに行く	私は泳ぎに行きます。 彼は飲みに行きました。 彼女は買い物しに行きたい。	*I'm going swimming.* *He went drinking.* *She wants to go shopping.*	**go ...ing**
その他	それから ... 何もすることがないよ。 やることがあります。 間違った！	*After that ...* *I'm not doing anything.* *I'm doing something.* *I made a mistake.*	**Other**

You got it? (分かった？)

☺

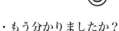

Yes
OR
No

☹

- もう分かりましたか？
- チャレンジをやってみよう。
- *3f, 3g & 3h (ページ28~30)*にトライしよう。

- まだ分かりませんか？
- まず、*3b, 3c, 3d & 3e*を読んで*(ページ22~27)*
- *3f, 3g & 3h (ページ28~30)*にトライしよう。

- ***You got it?***
- ***Try the challenge section:***
- ***Exercises 3f, 3g, 3h (pages 28~30)***

- ***You don't get it? Not sure?***
- ***Read Sections 3b, 3c, 3d & 3e (pages 22~27)***
- ***Then, try exercises 3f, 3g, 3h (pages 28~30)***

THE ENGLISH STORY

Making Plans - Yoko and John talk about their plans.

1 John: *Did you enjoy the barbecue, Yoko?*

2 Yoko: *Yeah.*[1] *I really had a good time, thanks.*

3 John: *How about you, Paul? Did you enjoy yourself?*

4 Paul: *Yep. It was great!*

5 John: *Good. It's only 2 o'clock, so let's go back to my place.*

6 Paul: *I can't. I'm meeting Linda at 4 and we're going to the movies.*

7 John: *What about after that?*

8 Paul: *After that?*[2] *We're going to Linda's place.*

9 John: *I see. What about you, Yoko? What are you doing tonight?*[3]

10 Yoko: *I'm going swimming*[4] *with Ringo at 3.*

11 John: *With Ringo?*

12 Yoko: *Uh huh. Then we're playing cards with Mic and Keith.*

13 John: *And after that?*

14 Yoko: *After that I'm going out with Ray and Dave. We're going bowling and then we're meeting Lola for dinner.*

15 John: *What about after dinner?*

16 Yoko: *After dinner I'm watching a basketball game with Michael.*

17 John: *How about after the game?*

18 Yoko: *After the game I'm having a piano lesson with Stevie.*

19 John: *And after that?*

20 Yoko: *After that I'm not doing anything.*[5]

21 John: *Great. Would you like to . . . . .*

22 Yoko: *I'm sorry. I made a mistake.*[6] *I am doing something*[7] *after the piano lesson. I'm going to bed! See you later, guys!*[1]

Simon Says - Easy Conversational English

THE JAPANESE STORY

3c
予定

予定 - ヨーコとジョンは予定について話します。

1 ジョン: ヨーコ、バーベキューは楽しかった？

2 ヨーコ: うん、[1] ほんとうに楽しかったわ。（ありがとう。）

3 ジョン: ポールは？　楽しかったかい？

4 ポール: ああ、楽しかったよ。

5 ジョン: よかった。まだ２時だから、僕んち（僕の家）へ戻ろうよ。

6 ポール: だめなんだ。４時にリンダと会うんだ。一緒に映画に行くんだよ。

7 ジョン: そのあとは？[2]

8 ポール: そのあとかい？ リンダの家に行くよ。

9 ジョン: わかったよ。ヨーコはどう？ 今夜は何をするの？[3]（今夜の予定は？）

10 ヨーコ: ３時にリンゴと泳ぎに行くわ。[4]

11 ジョン: リンゴと？

12 ヨーコ: そうよ。それからミックとキースといっしょにカード（トランプ）をするの。

13 ジョン: で、そのあとは？

14 ヨーコ: そのあとは、レイとデイヴと出掛けるわ。ボウリングに行くのよ。それからローラと会って食事（夕食）に行くの。

15 ジョン: 食事のあとは？

16 ヨーコ: 食事のあとは、マイケルといっしょにバスケ（ットボール）の試合を見るの。

17 ジョン: 試合のあとは？

18 ヨーコ: 試合のあとは、スティービーとピアノのレッスンよ。

19 ジョン: それでそのあとは？

20 ヨーコ: そのあとは何もすることがないわ。[5]（何も予定はないわ。）

21 ジョン: いいねえ。あのさ、もしよければ．．．

22 ヨーコ: あ、ごめんなさい！間違えちゃった。[6] ピアノのレッスンのあと、することがあったわ。[7] 寝るんだったわ。じゃあまたね！

3d
予定

Simon Says - Easy Conversational English

EXAMPLES

A: You hungry, Jack?
B: Nah, I just ate a mac, Donald.
How 'bout you?
A: Yeah. I want a burger.

* * *

A: What are you doing tonight, Frank?
B: I'm going out with Emma.

* * *

A: What you doing tomorrow, Freddie?
B: I'm going to the opera.

* * *

A: What you gonna eat for dinner?
B: I'm not gonna eat anything.
I'm on a diet.

* * *

A: You wanna go swimming?
B: Nope. I went swimming yesterday.
Let's go bowling!

* * *

A: You forgot my birthday!
B: Sorry. I made a mistake.
I thought it was tomorrow.

* * *

A: You wanna play video games tonight?
B: Nah, sorry. I'm doing something.
A: OK. How about tomorrow night?
B: Sounds good. I'm not doing anything.

A: ジャック、お腹空いてる？
B: いやあ、マックを食べたばっかり。
ドナルドは？
B: うん、バーガー食べたいなあ。

* * *

A: フランク、今晩は何するの？
B: エマとデートだよ。

* * *

A: フレディ、明日は何するの？
B: オペラに行くよ。

* * *

A: 晩飯は何を食うの？
B: 何も食わないよ。
今はダイエット中なんだ。

* * *

A: 泳ぎに行かない？
B: ううん。昨日泳ぎに行ったんだ。
ボーリングしに行こうよ。

* * *

A: 私の誕生日を忘れたでしょう。
B: ごめん。間違った。
明日だと思ってた...

* * *

A: 今晩ゲームやらない？
B: ううん。ごめん。用事があるんだ。
A: 分かった。明日の夜は？
B: いいよ。明日は用事がないよ。

3e

予定

LEARN THESE SENTENCES

1   うん、はい   Yeah, yeah, yeah

Look at the diagram. Do you understand?

*Yes*と*No*はよく使われているけど、会話的な方も使ってみよう。好きな表現を使ってね。

標準日本語	標準英語	会話的
はい。	Yes	*Yeah* / *Yep* / *Uh-huh*
いいえ。	No	*Nah* / *Nope* / *Uh uh*

You like beer?

Yeah. I love it. How 'bout you?

Uh huh. Me too!

Do you speak French?

Nah. How 'bout you?

Nope. Me neither.

2   そのあとは。   After that,

Look at the diagram. Do you understand?

話の順番を分かりやすくするための言い方だよ。

標準日本語	標準英語	会話的
そのあとは	After that,	*After that,* / *Then,* / *Finally,*

例

秋葉原に行って、
<u>その後</u>新宿にも行って、
<u>それから</u>浅草に寄って、
<u>最後に</u>帰った。

→ *We went to Akiba, <u>after that</u> Shinjuku, <u>then</u> Asakusa, and <u>finally</u> we went home.*

So, where did you go?

Well, I went to Paris.

Then, I went to Rome.

After that, I went to Venice.

Finally, I came back to Japan.

3   今晩どう(何)するの？   What are you doing tonight?

Look at the diagram. Do you understand?

標準日本語	標準英語	会話的
今晩どうするの？ ...何するの？	What are you going to do tonight?	*What are you doing tonight?* / *What (are) you gonna do tonight?*

Hey John, What are you doing tonight?

I'm drinking beer tonight.

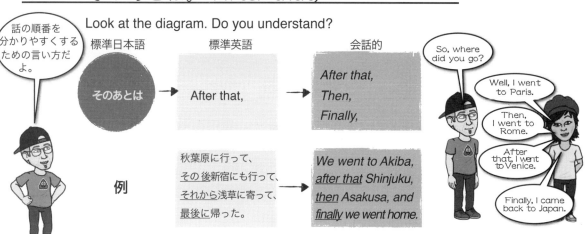

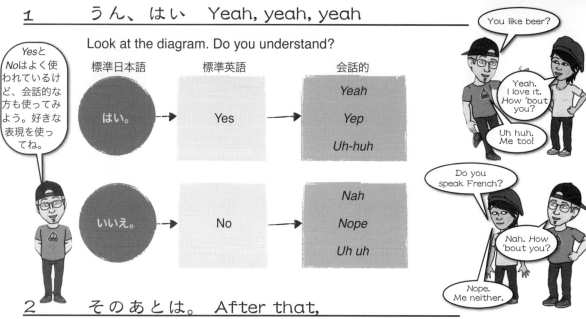

LEARN THESE SENTENCES

Can you see the patterns? Look at these examples.

	標準英語		会話的
パターン1	I am going to eat. He is going to play. We are going to jog. John is going to work.	→	*I'm eating.* *He's playing.* *We're jogging.* *John's working.*
例1	今週末、誰に会いますか？	→	*Who are you meeting this weekend?*
例2	今週末、彼女に会います。	→	*I am meeting my girlfriend this weekend.*
例3	今週末、誰にも会いません。	→	*I am not meeting anybody this weekend.*
パターン2	I am going to eat. He is going to play. We are going to jog. John is going to work.	→	*I'm gonna eat.* *He's gonna play.* *We're gonna jog.* *John's gonna work.*
例4	今週末、誰に会うの？	→	*Who are you gonna meet this weekend?*
例5	今週末、彼女に会うよ。	→	*I am gonna meet my girlfriend this weekend.*
例6	今週末、誰にも会わない。	→	*I am not gonna meet anybody this weekend.*

What are you doing tonight?
I'm watching TV.

Where are you going in Golden Week?
I'm going to Seoul.

Are you working tonight?
Nah, I'm not working tonight.

What are you gonna buy?
I'm gonna buy some tissues.

You gonna see your boyfriend tonight?
Nope. I'm not gonna see him again.

LEARN THESE SENTENCES

4　泳ぎに行きます。　I'm going swimming.

Look at the diagram. Do you understand?

標準日本語	標準英語	会話的
泳ぎに行く	I am going to go swimming.	I'm going swimming.

go＋
スポーツ・
趣味が多いよ。

例	泳ぎに行こう。 泳ぎに行きました。 泳ぎに行きたい。 泳ぎに行ったことがある。 泳ぎに行きます。	Let's go swimming. I went swimming. I want to go swimming. I have been swimming. I'm going swimming.
例	買い物しに行く 飲みに行く スキーしに行く ボーリングしに行く 釣りしに行く	go shopping go drinking go skiing go bowling go fishing

Wanna go bowling?

No. I'm going shopping.

Let's go dancing?

I don't want to go dancing.

5&7　用事がある・ない。　I'm (not) doing anything/something.

Look at the diagram. Do you understand?

質問（日本語）	答え（日本語）	答え（英語）
用事がある？	ううん、用事がない。	Nah, I'm not doing anything.
	はい、用事がある。	Yeah, I'm doing something.

よく
ある言い方
だよ。

You busy tonight?

Yeah, I'm doing something.

6　間違った。　I made a mistake.

Look at the diagram. Do you understand?

標準日本語	標準英語	会話的
間違った。	I made a mistake.	same

I mistakedとかI mistookとか
I mistakeと言わないでね。

Hi Emi.

I'm not Emi !

Sorry. I made a mistake...

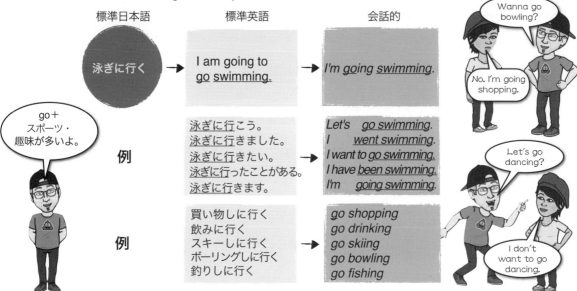

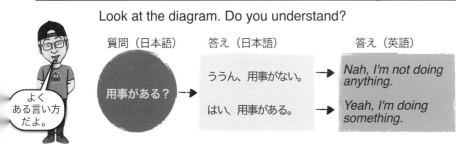

3f
予定

CHALLENGE STAGE

Challenge 1. *Fill in the blanks from the list.*

1 Hideki: Did you enjoy the barbecue, Ichiro?

2 Ichiro: Yep. 楽しかった。

3 Hideki: How about you Hideo? 楽しかった？

4 Hideo: Yeah. It was really good.

5 Hideki: Great. It's only about 3, so let's go watch a DVD.

6 Ichiro: できない。 I'm meeting Daisuke at 4.

7 Hideki: そのあとは？

8 Ichiro: After that? We're going to watch baseball.

9 Hideki: I see. ヒデオさんは？

10 Hideo: I'm going jogging with Shohei.

11 Hideki: With Shohei?

12 Hideo: うん、ショウヘイさんと。 Then we're going to the gym with Tomo.

13 Hideki: ジムのあとは？

14 Hideo: After that, I'm having dinner with Sadaharu.

15 Hideki: サダハルさんと食事のあとは？

16 Hideo: After that, I'm not doing anything.

17 Hideki: You sure are busy, Hideo.

Choose the best sentence for the blanks:

a) And after that?
b) Yep, with Shohei.
c) What about after the gym?
d) Did you enjoy yourself?
e) I had a really good time, thanks.
f) I can't.
g) And after dinner with Sadaharu?
h) What about you, Hideo?

3g
予定

CHALLENGE STAGE

Challenge 2. *Circle the correct answer.*

1. Which expression means *No*?
   (a) Note. (b) Nose.
   (c) Node. (d) Nope.

2. Which expression means *Yes*?
   (a) Yap. (b) Yop.
   (c) Yip. (d) Yep.

3. Fill-in the blank. *I'm meeting Paul at 3. _ _ _ _ _ _ we're going to the movies.*
   (a) After then, (b) After that,
   (c) That after, (d) Then after,

4. Jack wants to go to a dance with Jill on Friday. What does he say?
   (a) Let's go to dance on Friday. (b) Let's going dancing on Friday.
   (c) Let's go at dance on Friday. (d) Let's go dancing on Friday.

5. *Heh Joe. What are you doing tomorrow?* The best answer is:
   (a) I'm go to a concert with Jimi. (b) I going to a concert with Jimi.
   (c) I go to a concert with Jimi. (d) I'm going to a concert with Jimi.

6. You went to a department store with your friend yesterday and bought many things. What can you say?
   (a) We went shopping yesterday. (b) We go shopping yesterday.
   (c) We went shopped yesterday. (d) We go shopped yesterday.

7. Which sentence means the same as *I am going to go fishing on Sunday.*
   (a) I gonna go fish on Sunday. (b) I'm gonna fishing on Sunday.
   (c) I gonna go fishing on Sunday. (d) I'm gonna go fishing on Sunday.

8. *Are you busy tomorrow night?* If you have no plans, you say:
   (a) I'm not doing nothing. (b) I'm doing something.
   (c) I'm not doing anything. (d) I'm doing anything.

9. If you do the wrong thing, or say the wrong thing, you should say:
   (a) I mistaked. (b) I made a mistake.
   (c) I mistook. (d) I am a mistake.

10. You will buy a new TV next month. Which sentence is NOT the same?
    (a) I bought a new TV next month. (b) I'm gonna buy a new TV next month.
    (c) I'm buying a new TV next month. (d) I'm going to buy a new TV next month.

CHALLENGE STAGE

Challenge 3. *Did you read the English story?*
Let's check!

1. Did Yoko and Paul enjoy the barbecue?
   (i) Yes, they did.
   (ii) No, they didn't.
   (iii) Yes, they didn't.
   (iv) No, they did.

2. Who is Paul meeting at 4 o'clock?
   (i) He's meeting John.
   (ii) He's meeting Stevie.
   (iii) He's meeting Ringo.
   (iv) He's meeting Linda.

3. What is Paul doing after going to the movies?
   (i) He is going bowling.
   (ii) He is going to Linda's place.
   (iii) He is playing cards.
   (iv) He is having a piano lesson.

4. Who is Yoko going swimming with?
   (i) She's going swimming with John.
   (ii) She's going swimming with Linda.
   (iii) She's going swimming with Ringo.
   (iv) She's going swimming by herself.

5. Who are Yoko and Ringo going to play cards with?
   (i) They are playing cards by themselves.
   (ii) They are playing cards with John and Paul.
   (iii) They are playing cards with Ray and Dave.
   (iv) They are playing cards with Mic and Keith.

6. Who is Yoko going bowling with?
   (i) Yoko is going bowling with Paul.
   (ii) Yoko is going bowling with Ringo.
   (iii) Yoko is going bowling with Lola.
   (iv) Yoko is going bowling with Ray and Dave.

7. Who is Yoko meeting for dinner?
   (i) She's meeting Lola for dinner.
   (ii) She's meeting Michael for dinner.
   (iii) She's meeting Stevie for dinner.
   (iv) She's meeting John for dinner.

8. What are Yoko and Michael going to do together?
   (i) They are playing cards.
   (ii) They are watching a basketball game.
   (iii) They are going swimming.
   (iv) They are having a barbecue (bbq).

9. Who is Yoko going to have a piano lesson with?
   (i) She's having a piano lesson with Stevie.
   (ii) She's having a piano lesson with Ringo.
   (iii) She's having a piano lesson with Paul.
   (iv) She's having a piano lesson with Mic.

10. What is Yoko doing after she finishes her piano lesson?
   (i) After her lesson, she's going drinking.
   (ii) After her lesson, she's going to bed.
   (iii) After her lesson, she's reading a book.
   (iv) After her lesson, she's going swimming.

"Let's go out!"

あの、金曜日に一緒に映画を見に行きませんか。

うん。喜んで。

Um, would you like to go watch a movie with me on Friday?

Yeah, I'd love to.

QUICK START

招待	一緒に ... しませんか。	Would you like to ... ?	Inviting
	... をご一緒に出来たら幸いです。	I was wondering if you'd ...	
	一緒に ... しましょう。	Let's ...	

受け方	喜んで（...します）。	I'd love to.	Accepting
	いいですね。	(That) sounds great/good.	
	いいですね。	(That) sounds like fun.	

断り方	出来たら良いですが...	I wish I could but ...	Declining
	誘ってくれて嬉しいですが ...	Thanks for inviting me but ...	
	残念だけど、できないんだ。	I'm sorry but I can't.	

その他	あの、えーと、あのね	Well, let me see, umm	Other
	７時半にしましょう。	Let's make it 7:30.	
	楽しみにしています。	I'm looking forward to it.	
	楽しみにしてる。	I can't wait!	
	当たり前だよ。	No wonder!	

You got it? (分かった？)

☺   ☹

   Yes OR No

・もう分かりましたか？
・チャレンジをやってみよう
・4f, 4g & 4h (ページ38~40)にトライしよう。

・まだ分かりませんか？
・まず、4b, 4c, 4d & 4eを読んで(ページ32~37)
・4f, 4g & 4h (ページ38~40)にトライしよう。

・You got it?
・Try the challenge section:
・Exercises 4f, 4g, 4h (pages 38~40)

・You don't get it? Not sure?
・Read Sections 4b, 4c, 4d & 4e (pages 32~37)
・Then, try exercises 4f, 4g, 4h (pages 38~40)

4b
招待

THE ENGLISH STORY

Invitations - John invites Yoko out for dinner.

1 John: *Hi Yoko. Er [1] ... how've you been?*

2 Yoko: *Not bad, but I'm a bit tired.*

3 John: *No wonder! [2] You were doing something every day last week.*

4 Yoko: *Yeah. I've been pretty busy recently.*

5 John: *Actually, there's ... um ... something I want to ask you.*

6 Yoko: *Sure.*

7 John: *Well ... I was wondering if ... ah ... I was wondering if ...*

8 Yoko: *Yeah, what?*

9 John: *Well ... I was wondering if you would like to ... let me see ... well ... if you would like to go out with me on Friday night. [3]*

10 Yoko: *I'm sorry John. I didn't catch what you said. Could you say it again please?*

11 John: *Sure. Umm ... I said ... I was wondering if ... ah ... if you would like to ... er ... go out with me on Friday night.*

12 Yoko: *Yeah, I'd love to! [4]*

13 John: *Great! I know a really nice ethnic restaurant and the food is really tasty.*

14 Yoko: *It sounds really good. Ahh ... what time?*

15 John: *Ah ... how about 7:00?*

16 Yoko: *I'm working till 6:00. Umm ... 7:30 is better for me.*

17 John: *Okay. Let's make it 7:30. [5]*

18 Yoko: *Yep, that's good.*

19 John: *Great! I'll pick you up in front of your apartment at 7:30. OK?*

20 Yoko: *Sure! I'm really looking forward to it. [6]*

21 John: *Me too. Ah ... See you on Friday!*

22 Yoko: *Okay John. See you then!*

THE JAPANESE STORY

4c
招待

招待 - ジョンはヨーコを外食に誘います。

1 ジョン: やあ、ヨーコ。あの ...[1] 元気にしていたかい？

2 ヨーコ: まあまあね。でもちょっと疲れてるの。

3 ジョン: 当然じゃない！[2] 先週は毎日何か予定があったじゃないか。

4 ヨーコ: そうね。最近は結構忙しくしているわ。

5 ジョン: 実はさあ、ちょっと ... あのさ ... 君に聞きたいことがあるんだよ。

6 ヨーコ: いいわよ。

7 ジョン: ええと ... もしよければ ... あの ... もし君がよければ ...

8 ヨーコ: ええ、なあに？

9 ジョン: あの ... もし君がよければ ... あのね ... その ... もし君がよければ、金曜の夜に僕とデートしてくれないかな？[3]

10 ヨーコ: ごめんなさい、ジョン。何て言ったのか聞き取れなかったの。もう一度言ってくれる？

11 ジョン: うん。あの ... もし ... 君がよければ ... 金曜の夜に ... 僕と ... デート ... しないかい ... って ... 言ったんだよ ...

12 ヨーコ: いいわよ。喜んで！[4]

13 ジョン: やった！　すっごくいいエスニック・レストランを知ってるんだ。ほんとうにおいしいんだよ。

14 ヨーコ: 楽しみだわ。ええと ... 何時に？

15 ジョン: そうだな ... 7時でどうかな？

16 ヨーコ: 私は6時まで仕事をしているから ... 7時半の方が都合がいいんだけれど。

17 ジョン: じゃあ7時半にしよう。[5]

18 ヨーコ: ええ、それでいいわ。

19 ジョン: いいね。ええと ... 7時半に君のアパートに迎えに行くよ。いいかい？

20 ヨーコ: いいわ。楽しみにしているわね。[6]

21 ジョン: 僕もだよ。あ ... じゃあ金曜にね！

22 ヨーコ: オーケー、ジョン。じゃあまたね。

4d 招待

A: *Ted, would you like to go to the movies with us on Friday?*
B: *Yeah, sounds like fun!*
A: *How 'bout you Bill?*
C: *I'm sorry but I can't. I have to finish my homework on Friday.*

* * *

A: *Mic, I was wondering if you'd like to go to the concert tonight.*
B: *Thanks for inviting me but I'm meeting my girlfriend tonight.*
A: *What about you Keith?*
C: *Thanks! I'd love to!*

* * *

A: *Let's buy some beers and chill!*
B: *Yep. Sounds good.*

* * *

A: *You looking forward to Christmas?*
B: *Sure. I can't wait.*

* * *

A: *Umm ... Let me see ...*
Is your name ... er ... Paul?
B: *No Dad. I'm John!*

* * *

A: *When do you want to get married?*
B: *In the summer.*
A: *OK. Let's make it June!*

A: テッド、金曜日に僕たちと一緒に映画を見に行かない？
B: うん。いいですね。
A: ビルは？
C: ごめん。出来ないよ。金曜日に宿題を終らせないと...

* * *

A: ミック、もし良ければ、今晩のコンサートに一緒に行きませんか？
B: 誘ってくれて嬉しいですが、今晩彼女に会う予定です。
A: じゃ、キースは？
C: ありがとう！ 喜んで！

* * *

A: ビールを買って、ゆっくりしよう！
B: うん。いいね。

* * *

A: クリスマスを楽しみにしていますか？
B: うん。楽しみしてる。(待ってられない。)

* * *

A: あのー、えーっと、あの、あ、あなたの ... 名前 ... ポールですよね？
B: お父さん、違うよー。僕ジョンだよ！

* * *

A: いつ結婚したいですか？
B: 夏が良いですね。
A: じゃ、6月にしましょう！

LEARN THESE SENTENCES

1　あの、えーと、あのね　Well, let me see, um...

Ah...Wanna go bowling?
Let me see... Nah. I'm busy.

Look at the diagram. Do you understand?

	日本語	英語
あいづち →	あの ... えーと ... あのね ... →	Well ... Umm ... Ah ... Er ... Hmm ... Let me see ...
例	お母さん、あの ... お金を ... えーと ... ちょっと ... あの ... 貸してくれますか？ →	*Mum, well ... could you ... er ... lend me umm ... some money.*

あいづちを使うと会話はスムースになるよ。
特に恥ずかしい話や言いにくいことによく使われてるよ。

Um . . . Let's go dancing!
Well ... I can't ... er ... dance.

2　当たり前！　No wonder!

Look at the diagram. Do you understand?

標準日本語	標準英語	会話的
当たり前！（当然） →	It's no wonder! Obviously! →	*No wonder!*

I'm tired!!
No wonder! You didn't sleep last night!

3/4　誘い方・受け方・断り方　Invitations

Look at the diagram. Do you understand?
There are 3 invitations, 3 acceptances and 3 refusals.
（招待の誘い方、受け方、断り方は３つずつあります。よく見て。）

色々な誘い方があるけど、この３つを覚えよう。

招待のキーワード	受け方のキーワード	断り方のキーワード
I was wondering . . . Would you like to . . . Let's . . . →	I'd love to. Sounds good,nice, great, wonderful, fantastic, cool. Sounds like fun. →	*Sorry but I can't.* *I wish I could but ...* *Thanks for inviting me but ...*

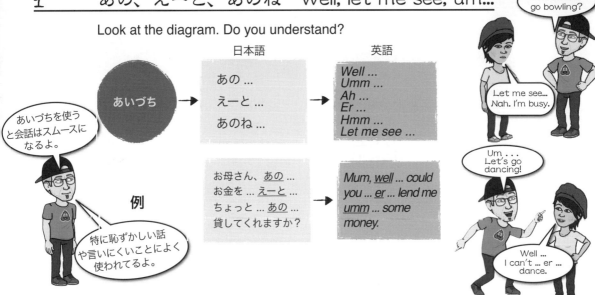

Would you like to watch a movie with me?
Sounds great!

LEARN THESE SENTENCES

There are three (3) easy patterns. Look at the examples.

		日本語	会話的英語
誘い方	1	もし良ければ、一緒に...をしませんか？	I was wondering if you'd like to ...
	2	...一緒にしませんか？	Would you like to ...
	3	...にしましょう。	Let's ...
丁寧	1	もし良ければ、金曜日に私と一緒にボーリングしに行きませんか？	I was wondering if you'd like to go bowling with me on Friday.
普通	2	金曜日に私と一緒にボーリングしに行きませんか？	Would you like to go bowling with me on Friday?
フレンドリー	3	ボーリングしに行こう！	Let's go bowling on Friday.

受け方	1	喜んで。	I'd love to.
	2	いいですね。	(That) sounds good.
	3	おもしろそうですね。	(That) sounds like fun.
丁寧	1	喜んで。	I'd love to!
普通 1	2	いいですね！	(That) sounds good. / " great. / " cool. / " nice.
普通 2	3	おもしろそうですね。	(That) sounds like fun. or (That) sounds fun.

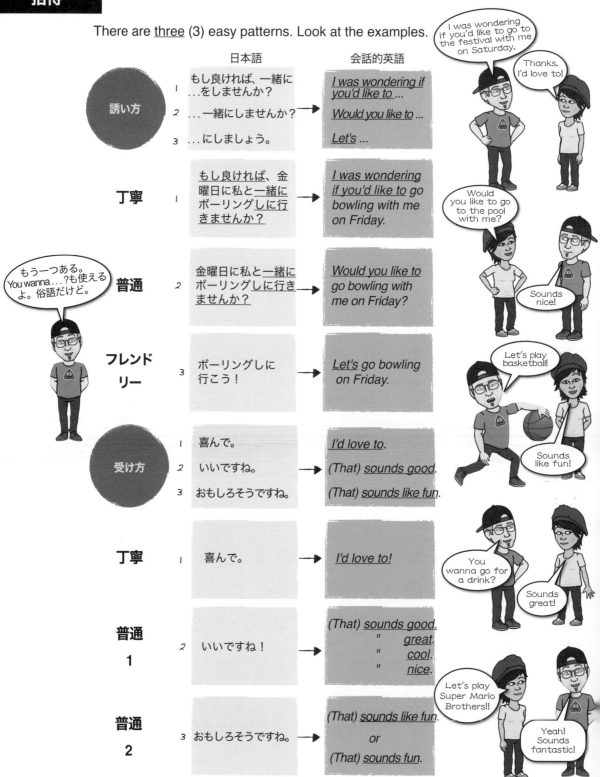

LEARN THESE SENTENCES

There are three easy patterns for refusing an invitation. Look at the examples.

	日本語	会話的英語
断り方	出来たら良いのですが...	*I wish I could but ...*
	誘ってくれて嬉しいですが...	*Thanks for inviting me but ...*
	すみませんが、ちょっと	*I'm sorry, but I can't ...*

普通 1   1 出来たら良いのですがレポートを書かないと。 → *I wish I could but I have to write a report.*

普通 2   2 誘ってくれて嬉しいですが、今晩お母さんと会うんです。 → *Thanks for inviting me but I'm meeting my mother tonight.*

普通 3   3 ごめん。出来ない。歯医者さんに行かないと。 → *Sorry, but I can't. I have to go to the dentist.*

忘れないで。断ると理由も言わないと...

Let's go watch a movie!

Sorry. I wish I could but I have to wash my clothes.

You wanna go to karaoke with me?

Thanks for inviting me but I'm meeting Paul tonight.

5   7時半にしましょう。   <u>Let's make it 7:30.</u>

Look at the diagram. Do you understand?

標準日本語	標準英語	会話的
7時半にしよう。	Let's make it 7:30.	*same*

What time shall we start the bbq?

Well, I'm working till 6.

So let's make it 7:30. OK?

6   楽しみにしています。   <u>I'm looking forward to it.</u>

Look at the diagram. Do you understand?

標準日本語	標準英語	会話的
楽しみにしています。	I'm looking forward to it.	*I can't wait.* *I'm looking forward to it.*

Don't forget. Party tomorrow night!

I can't wait!!

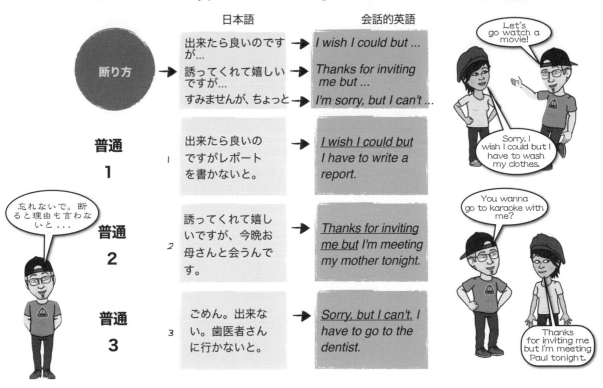

CHALLENGE STAGE

Challenge 1. *Fill in the blanks from the list.*

1 Jack: Hi Jill. 元気でしたか？

2 Jill: Okay, but I'm a bit tired.

3 Jack: 当然じゃない！ You were really busy last week.

4 Jill: Yep. 最近、忙しいんですよね。

5 Jack: Actually, there's something I want to ask you.

6 Jill: Sure.

7 Jack: Well, would you like to ... um ... would you like to go up the hill with me on Sunday?

8 Jill: I'm sorry Jack. 言ったことが聞き取れなかったんだけど。 Could you repeat it again please?

9 Jack: Sure. あの... 日曜日に山登りへ一緒に行きませんか、と言ったんですよ。

10 Jill: Yeah, 喜んで！

11 Jack: Great! I'll pick you up at your house at 8:00. Okay?

12 Jill: Sure. 楽しみに待っています。

13 Jack: Me too! Umm ... See you on Sunday!

14 Jill: Okay Jack. またね！

Choose the best sentence for the blanks:

a) No wonder!

b) See you then!

c) How have you been?

d) I said I was wondering if you'd like to go up the hill with me on Sunday.

e) I didn't catch what you said.

f) I've been pretty busy recently.

g) I'd love to!

h) I'm really looking forward to it.

4g
招待

CHALLENGE STAGE

Challenge 2. *Circle the correct answer.*

1. Which sentences is NOT good? (良くないあいづち)
   (a) Are you ... um ... French? (b) Are you ... let me see ... French?
   (c) Are you ... er ... French? (d) Are you ... ano ... French?

2. John says *I ate 4 large pizzas. I feel sick!* (具合が悪い！) What do you say to him?
   (a) No window! (b) No wandering!
   (c) No wonder! (d) No chunder!

3. Which is NOT an invitation? (招待じゃない)
   (a) Would you like to go fishing? (b) Let's go fishing.
   (c) You wanna go fishing? (d) Do you like fishing?

4. Which is NOT a good way of accepting an invitation? (良くない受け方)
   (a) I'd love to! (b) That sounds good!
   (c) That sounds like fun! (d) That sounds foolish!

5. Which is NOT a good way of declining an invitation? (良くない断り方)
   (a) I'm sorry but I can't... (b) Thanks for inviting me but...
   (c) I wish I could but ... (d) I don't want an invitation.

6. Which of the following is NOT a good reason for declining an invitation? (良くない理由)
   Thanks for inviting me but
   (a) I have to work. (b) I have a dog.
   (c) I'm meeting my father. (d) I have to write my report.

7. Your friend says *What time shall we start the bbq?* You want to begin at 6PM, so you say:
   (a) Let's on 6:00. (b) Let's decide at 6:00.
   (c) Let's decide for 6:00. (d) Let's make it 6:00.

8. Which question is an easy way to invite your friend to bowling?
   (a) You want bowling? (b) You bowling?
   (c) You wanna go bowling? (d) Can you bowling?

9. There is a live concert tomorrow night. You want to go. (楽しみに待ってる！)
   (a) I'm looking for the concert! (b) I'm looking over the concert!
   (c) I'm looking at the concert! (d) I'm looking forward to the concert!

10. Your vacation begins soon. You are very excited. What do you say? (すごく楽しみにしてる！)
    (a) I'm waiting! (b) I can wait!
    (c) I'm not waiting (d) I can't wait!

CHALLENGE STAGE

Challenge 3. Did you read the English story?
Let's check!

1. How has Yoko been recently?
   - *(i)* *She has been busy.*
   - *(ii)* *She has been working.*
   - *(iii)* *She has been sad.*
   - *(iv)* *She has been lonely.*

2. Is Yoko tired?
   - *(i)* *She's really tired.*
   - *(ii)* *She's very tired.*
   - *(iii)* *She's a bit tired.*
   - *(iv)* *She's not tired.*

3. What does John want to ask Yoko?
   - *(i)* *He wants to invite her to a restaurant.*
   - *(ii)* *He wants to invite her to the movies.*
   - *(iii)* *He wants to invite her for a drive.*
   - *(iv)* *He wants to invite her to karaoke.*

4. When is John's date?
   - *(i)* *It's Friday afternoon.*
   - *(ii)* *It's Friday night.*
   - *(iii)* *It's Saturday afternoon.*
   - *(iv)* *It's Saturday night.*

5. What does John know?
   - *(i)* *He knows Yoko's birthday.*
   - *(ii)* *He knows Yoko's mother.*
   - *(iii)* *He knows a nice ethnic restaurant.*
   - *(iv)* *He doesn't know anything.*

6. What does John say about the food?
   - *(i)* *He says the food is really hot.*
   - *(ii)* *He says the food is really cheap.*
   - *(iii)* *He says the food is really expensive.*
   - *(iv)* *He says the food is really tasty.*

7. What time is Yoko working until?
   - *(i)* *She's working until 5 o'clock.*
   - *(ii)* *She's working until 6 o'clock.*
   - *(iii)* *She's working until 7 o'clock.*
   - *(iv)* *She's not working.*

8. At first, what time does John want to pick up Yoko?
   - *(i)* *He wants to pick her up at 6 o'clock.*
   - *(ii)* *He wants to pick her up at 6:30.*
   - *(iii)* *He wants to pick her up at 7 o'clock.*
   - *(iv)* *He wants to pick her up at 7:30.*

9. What time does John pick up Yoko?
   - *(i)* *He picks her up at 6 o'clock.*
   - *(ii)* *He picks her up at 6:30.*
   - *(iii)* *He picks her up at 7 o'clock.*
   - *(iv)* *He picks her up at 7:30.*

10. Where does John pick up Yoko?
    - *(i)* *He picks her up at work.*
    - *(ii)* *He picks her up in front of her apartment.*
    - *(iii)* *He picks her up in the city.*
    - *(iv)* *He picks her up at his house.*

"What can I get you?"

5a
外食

QUICK START

店	ご注文はお決まりですか？ ご注文、よろしいでしょうか？	*Are you ready to order?* *May I take your order?* *What can I get you?* *What would you like?*	**Restaurant**
客	...にします。 ...をください。 ...をもらえますか。	*I'll have ... / I'd like ... / I'll take ...* *Can I get ... ? / Give me ...* *Could you get / bring ... ?*	**Customer**
いかが	...いかがですか？ 何か飲みませんか？ ...はどうですか？	*Would you like ... ?* *Would you like something to drink?* *How about a / some ... ?*	**Would you like**
その他	結構です。 他に何か？ なんか変です。 おいしそう！	*That's all. / That's fine.* *Anything else?/ (Is) that all?* *It's kinda' weird.* *Yum!*	**Other**

You got it? (分かった？)

☺

☹

・もう分かりましたか？
・チャレンジをやってみよう。
・*5f, 5g & 5h* (ページ*48~50*)にトライしよう。

・*You got it?*
・*Try the challenge section:*
・*Exercises 5f, 5g, 5h (pages 48~50)*

・まだ分かりませんか？
・まず、*5b, 5c, 5d & 5e*を読んで(ページ*42~47*)
・*5f, 5g & 5h* (ページ*48~50*)にトライしよう。

・*You don't get it? Not sure?*
・*Read Sections 5b, 5c, 5d & 5e (pages 42~47)*
・*Then, try exercises 5f, 5g, 5h (pages 48~50)*

5b
外食

THE ENGLISH STORY

Eating Out - John invites Yoko out for dinner.

1 John: *Well Yoko, how do you like the restaurant?*

2 Yoko: *Hmm. It's kinda' weird![1]*

3 John: *Yeah, I guess so, but it's famous and the food's really good.*

4 Yoko: *Great! I'm really hungry!*

5 John: *Look Yoko! Here comes the waiter.*

6 Yoko: *He looks like Dracula!*

7 John: *Of course! The restaurant's name is Dracula's!*

8 Waiter: *Are you ready to order,[2] sir?*

9 John: *Umm . . . what is today's special?*

10 Waiter: *It's garlic steak.*

11 Yoko: *Yum![3] I love garlic!*

12 John: *How is it cooked?*

13 Waiter: *It's pan fried. It's one of our specialities.*

14 Yoko: *Sounds good! I'll take the garlic steak![4]*

15 Waiter: *How would you like your steak, madam?*

16 Yoko: *Medium rare, please.*

17 Waiter: *And would you like vegetables or salad & french fries, madam?*

18 Yoko: *I'd like the salad and french fries, thank you.*

19 John: *And I'll take the roast beef, please.*

20 Waiter: *Certainly, sir. Would you like an appetizer or entree?[5]*

21 John: *Yes please, give us some garlic bread.*

22 Waiter: *Certainly, sir. Would you like something to drink?*

23 John: *I'll have a Bloody Mary...*

24 Yoko: *Could you bring me the wine list,[6] please.*

25 Waiter: *Certainly. Is there anything else?[7]*

26 John: *No thanks. That's fine.*

THE JAPANESE STORY

5c
外食

外食 - ジョンはヨーコを外食に誘います。

1 ジョン: ねえ、ヨーコ。このレストランはどう？
2 ヨーコ: そうねえ。なんか、ちょっと変な感じね。[1]
3 ジョン: うん、そうだね。でもここは有名だし、ほんとうに食事はおいしいんだよ。
4 ヨーコ: いいわね。私すごくお腹が空いてるのよ。
5 ジョン: ほらヨーコ！　ウェイターが来るよ。
6 ヨーコ: ドラキュラみたいね！
7 ジョン: もちろんさ。レストランの名前が「ドラキュラ」なんだよ。
8 ウェイター: お客様、ご注文はお決まりですか？[2]
9 ジョン: あの．．．今日のおすすめは何ですか？
10 ウェイター ガーリック・ステーキです。
11 ヨーコ: おいしそう！[3] ガーリックは大好きよ。
12 ジョン: 調理方法は？
13 ウェイター: フライパン焼きです。私どもの得意料理のひとつです。
14 ヨーコ: おいしそうね。私はガーリック・ステーキにするわ。[4]
15 ウェイター: ステーキはどのようになさいますか、お客様？
16 ヨーコ: ミディアム・レアにして下さい。
17 ウェイター: 野菜か、それともサラダとフライド・ポテト添えに致しますか？
18 ヨーコ: サラダとフライド・ポテトをお願いします。
19 ジョン: 僕はロースト・ビーフにするよ。
20 ウェイター: かしこまりました、お客様。前菜かアントレはいかがでしょうか？[5]
21 ジョン: そうだね、お願いしよう。ガーリック・ブレッドを少し下さい。
22 ウェイター: かしこまりました。何かお飲み物はいかがですか？
23 ジョン: 僕にはブラッディ・マリーを．．．
24 ヨーコ: ワインリストをもらえますか？[6]
25 ウェイター: かしこまりました。他に何かございますか？[7]
26 ヨーコ: いえ、これで結構です。

EXAMPLES

W: *Are you ready to order, sir?*
A: *Yes please. I'll have the steak.*
W: *Can I take your order, madam?*
B: *Uh-huh. I'd like the roast.*

*　*　*

W: *Would you like something to drink?*
A: *Yeah. I'll have a beer, thanks.*
W: *And you, madam?*
B: *Can I get a coke, please?*

*　*　*

A: *Could you get me an ashtray, please?*
W: *Certainly, sir.*

*　*　*

A: *Could you bring our bill, please?*
W: *Certainly, sir.*

*　*　*

W: *Is that all, sir?*
A: *Yes thanks. That's fine.*

*　*　*

W: *Is there anything else?*
A: *No thanks. That's fine.*

*　*　*

A: *This ice-cream tastes great. Yum!*
B: *Mine's yummy too!*

*　*　*

A: *It's kinda' late. Shall we go home.*
B: *Yeah. I'm kinda' tired. Let's go.*

W: お客様、お決まりですか？
A: ええ、私はステーキにします。
W: 奥様、ご注文は？
B: 私はローストをお願いします。

*　*　*

W: 何かお飲み物はいかがですか？
A: うん。ビールにします。
W: 奥様は？
B: コーラを一杯ください。

*　*　*

A: 灰皿をもらえますか？
W: はい、かしこまりました。

*　*　*

A: 伝票をもらえますか？
W: はい、かしこまりました。

*　*　*

W: これでよろしいですか？
A: はい、結構です。

*　*　*

W: 他に何かございますか？
A: いいえ、結構です。

*　*　*

A: このアイスはおいしいよ。オイシイ！
B: 僕のアイスもおいしいよ。

*　*　*

A: ちょっと遅いですね。帰りましょうか？
B: うん。なんか疲れてるし。帰ろう！

LEARN THESE SENTENCES

1　なんか、ちょっと変だね。　It's kinda weird ...

Look at the diagram. Do you understand?

標準日本語		標準英語		会話的
ちょっと	→	a little	→	*a bit* *a little bit*
なんか	→	kind of	→	*kinda*

2　ご注文はお決まりですか！　Are you ready to order?

Look at the diagram. Do you understand?

		日本語		会話的な英語
ご注文	→	ご注文はお決まりですか？ ご注文は決まりましたか？	→	*Are you ready to order?* *May I take your order?* *Can I take your order?* *What would you like?* *What can I get you?*

標準	ご注文はお決まりですか？	→	*Are you ready to order?*
丁寧 1	ご注文をお伺いしてよろしいですか？	→	*May I take your order?*
丁寧 2	ご注文はお決まりでしょうか？	→	*Can I take your order?* *Could I take your order?*
フレンドリー 1	ご注文は？	→	*What would you like?*
フレンドリー 2	お決まりですか？	→	*What can I get you?* *Can I get you something?*

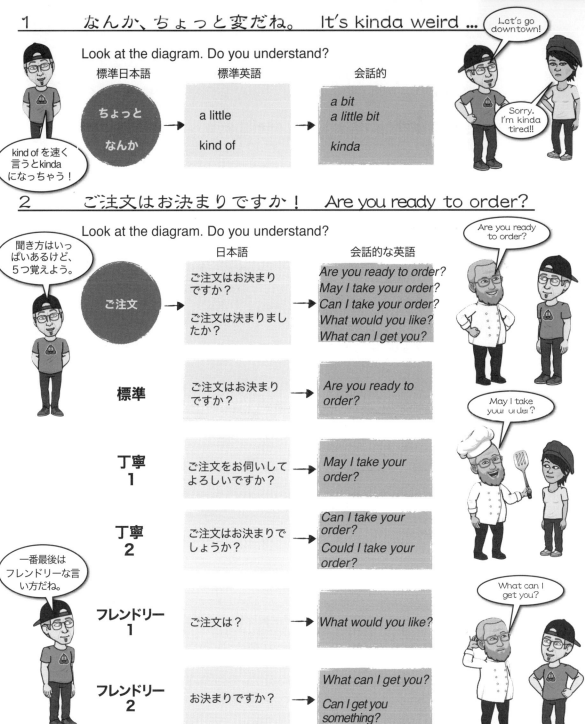

LEARN THESE SENTENCES

3　おいしい！　Yum! Yummy!

Look at the diagram. Do you understand?

標準日本語	標準英語	会話的
おいしい！ →	delicious →	*Yum* *Yummy* *Tastes good*

4　ステーキにします。　I'll take the steak.

Look at the diagram. Do you understand?

	日本語	会話的な英語
...にします。 →	...にします。 ...をお願いします。 ...をください。 →	*I'll take the ...* *I'll have the ...* *I'd like the ...* *Give me the ...* *Can I get the ...*
普通 1	...にします。 →	*I'll take the ...*
普通 2	...をお願いします。 →	*I'll have the ...*
普通 3	...をください。 →	*I'd like the ...*
命令用	...をくれ。 →	*Give me the ...*
フレンドリー	...をもらえますか？ →	*Can I get the ...*

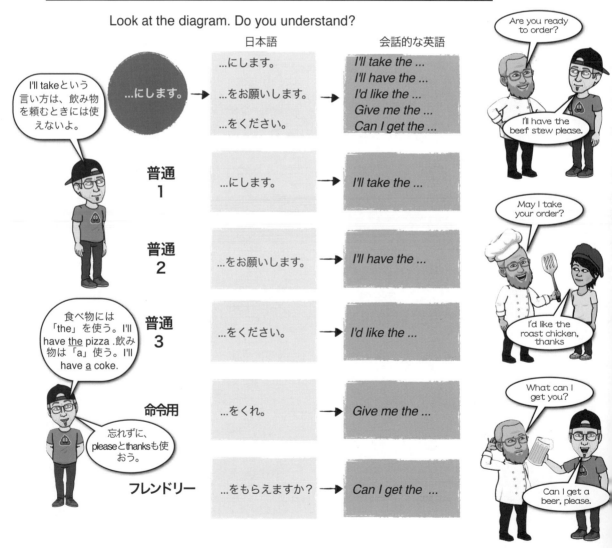

LEARN THESE SENTENCES

5 ...はいかがですか？ Would you like ...?

Look at the diagram. Do you understand?

標準日本語	標準英語	会話的
...いかがですか？ →	Would you like ... →	Would you like ... How about a/some...

	日本語	会話的英語
丁寧	コーヒーはいかがですか？ →	*Would you like a coffee?*
フレンドリー	コーヒーはどう？ 紅茶、飲む？ →	*How about a coffee?* *How about some tea?*

6 ...をもらえますか？ Could you bring ...?

Look at the diagram. Do you understand?

標準日本語	標準英語	会話的
...をもらえますか？ →	Could you bring ...? Could you get ...? Could I have ...? →	*Can/Could you bring ...?* *Can/Could you get ...?* *Can/Could/May I have ...?*

7 他に何か？ Is there anything else ...?

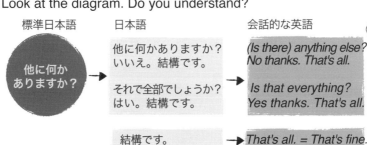

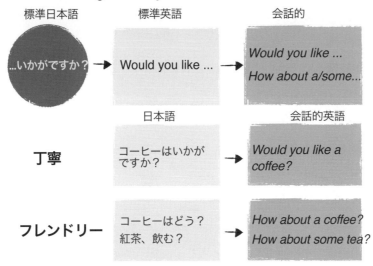

Look at the diagram. Do you understand?

標準日本語	日本語	会話的な英語
他に何かありますか？ →	他に何かありますか？ いいえ。結構です。 →	*(Is there) anything else?* *No thanks. That's all.*
	それで全部でしょうか？ はい。結構です。 →	*Is that everything?* *Yes thanks. That's all.*
	結構です。 →	*That's all. = That's fine.*

CHALLENGE STAGE

Challenge 1. *Fill in the blanks from the list.*

1 Jack: Well Rose, this restaurant opened last week. I wanted to come here.

2 Rose: Hmm. ちょっと高そうですが...

3 Jack: I read about it online. 料理はおいしいそうです。

4 Rose: Good. I'm really hungry!

5 Jack: Look Rose! Here comes the waiter.

6 Waiter: お決まりですか？

7 Jack: What do you recommend?

8 Waiter: Our vegetables are all organic. I recommend the green salad.

9 Rose: Sounds good! I love salads. 私はグリーンサラダにします。

10 Waiter: Certainly madam. 手作りドレッシングはいかがですか？

11 Rose: Yes, I'd like the homemade dressing, please.

12 Waiter: What can I get you sir?

13 Jack: フライド・フィッシュをお願いします。

14 Waiter: Certainly sir. お客様は何かお飲みになりますか？

15 Rose: 私、コーラをください。

16 Jack: ワインリストをもらえますか？

17 Waiter: Certainly sir. 他に何か？

18 Jack: No thanks. That's fine.

Choose the best sentence for the blanks:

a) I'll take the green salad, please.

b) It looks kinda expensive

c) I'll have a coke . . .

d) Would you like our homemade dressing?

e) Are you ready to order?

f) I'll take the fried fish, please.

g) Would you like something to drink?

h) Anything else?

i) Could you bring the wine list?

j) The food's really yummy.

CHALLENGE STAGE

Challenge 2. *Circle the correct answer.*

1. Which expression is similar to *I'm kinda hungry*?
   (a) I'm kind hungry. (b) I'm hungry kind.
   (c) I'm kind of hungry. (d) I'm a hungry kid.

2. The waiter says お決まりですか？ Which expression (表現) is NOT the same?
   (a) Are you giving me an order? (b) Are you ready to order?
   (c) May I take your order? (d) Can I take your order?

3. The waiter says *What can I get you?* Which expression (表現) is similar?
   (a) What can you get me? (b) What did you eat?
   (c) Are you hungry? (d) What would you like?

4. If you want to order a steak, which one of the following expressions is NOT good?
   (a) I'll have the steak. (b) Could you steak me, please?
   (c) Give me the steak, please. (d) I'll take the steak, please.

5. You want a beer. Which expression (表現) is similar to *Can I get a beer please?*
   (a) Are you giving me a beer? (b) Can I beer please?
   (c) Give me a beer please. (d) May you get a beer please?

6. Which drink order (注文) is NOT good?
   (a) Give me a coke. (b) I'll have a hot chocolate.
   (c) I'd like a glass of red wine. (d) I'll bring an orange juice please.

7. The waiter says *Would you like some edamame?* This is similar to:
   (a) How about some *edamame*? (b) Would you bring some *edamame*?
   (c) Do you like *edamame*? (d) Do you like some *edamame*?

8. You finish eating. The waiter says *Anything else?* You say「結構です。」Which answer is NOT good?
   (a) No. That's fine. (b) No. That's all.
   (c) No thanks. (d) Thank you.

9. You want the bill (伝票). Which expression is NOT good to say to the waiter?
   (a) Could you bring the bill? (b) May I have the bill?
   (c) Can I take the bill? (d) Could you get the bill?

10. If the food is really tasty, we can say:
    (a) Bummy! (b) Bimbo!
    (c) Yimbo! (d) Yummy!

5h
外食

CHALLENGE STAGE

Challenge 3. Did you read the English story?
Let's check!

1. Where did John and Yoko go for dinner?
   - *(i) They went to a Chinese restaurant.*
   - *(ii) They went to an Italian restaurant.*
   - *(iii) They went to a French restaurant.*
   - *(iv) They went to Dracula's restaurant.*

2. Is Yoko hungry?
   - *(i) Yes, she's a bit hungry.*
   - *(ii) Yes, she's very hungry.*
   - *(iii) Yes, she's really hungry.*
   - *(iv) No, she's not hungry.*

3. What main course does Yoko order?
   - *(i) She orders the garlic steak.*
   - *(ii) She orders the roast beef.*
   - *(iii) She orders the fried chicken.*
   - *(iv) She orders the pasta.*

4. What main course does John order?
   - *(i) He orders the garlic steak.*
   - *(ii) He orders the roast beef.*
   - *(iii) He orders the fried chicken.*
   - *(iv) He orders the pasta.*

5. How is the garlic steak cooked?
   - *(i) It's fried in a pan.*
   - *(ii) It's baked in an oven.*
   - *(iii) It's cooked on a barbecue.*
   - *(iv) It's boiled.*

6. What does Yoko order with her steak?
   - *(i) She orders nothing.*
   - *(ii) She orders vegetables.*
   - *(iii) She orders salad and french fries.*
   - *(iv) She orders beer.*

7. What appetizer (前菜) does John order?
   - *(i) He orders the garlic cheese.*
   - *(ii) He orders the garlic rice.*
   - *(iii) He orders the garlic chicken.*
   - *(iv) He orders the garlic bread.*

8. What drink does John order?
   - *(i) He orders a beer.*
   - *(ii) He orders a tomato juice.*
   - *(iii) He orders a coke.*
   - *(iv) He orders a Bloody Mary cocktail.*

9. What drink does Yoko ask for?
   - *(i) She asks for an orange juice.*
   - *(ii) She asks for a beer.*
   - *(iii) She asks for a glass of water.*
   - *(iv) She asks for the wine list.*

10. Who loves garlic?
    - *(i) John loves garlic.*
    - *(ii) Yoko loves garlic.*
    - *(iii) The waiter loves garlic.*
    - *(iv) Nobody loves garlic. It's stinky.*

6a 持っている

"Got any tissues?"

QUICK START

持つ	無料券を持っています。	I've got some free tickets?	have got
	お金がない。	I haven't got any money.	
	ティッシュはありますか？	Have you got any tissues?	
	ティッシュ、ある？	Got any tissues?	
どうぞ	はいどうぞ。	Here you are.	Here you are
	はいどうぞ。	Here you go.	
	どういたしまして。	No problem.	
	どういたしまして。	That's OK.	
意味	...ってどういう意味？	What does ... mean?	...mean...
	さっき言った言葉の意味は？	What do you mean by ...?	
	...というのは...という意味？	... means ...	
その他	... についてどう思う？	What do you think of ... ?	Other
	... についてどう思う？	How do you like ... ?	
	行かなければならない。	I have got to go.	
	行かなくちゃ！	I gotta go!	

You got it? (分かった？)

☺

・もう分かりましたか？
・チャレンジをやってみよう。
・*6f, 6g & 6h (ページ58~60)*にトライしよう。

・***You got it?***
・***Try the challenge section:***
・***Exercises 6f, 6g, 6h (pages 58~60)***

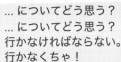

☹

・まだ分かりませんか？
・まず、*6b, 6c, 6d & 6e*を読んで*(ページ52~57)*
・*6f, 6g & 6h (ページ58~60)*にトライしよう。

・***You don't get it? Not sure?***
・***Read Sections 6b, 6c, 6d & 6e (pages 52~57)***
・***Then, try exercises 6f, 6g, 6h (pages 58~60)***

THE ENGLISH STORY

has got - John gives Yoko some free tickets.

1 John: *Hi Yoko. What did you think of the restaurant?* [1]
2 Yoko: *I really enjoyed the food. It was great!*
3 John: *Good. By the way, what are you doing tomorrow night?*
4 Yoko: *Tomorrow night? Nothing. Why?*
5 John: *Well ... I've got some free tickets* [2] *for a movie tomorrow night, but I'm busy, so I can't make it.*
6 Yoko: *What do you mean by* [3] *"I can't make it"? I don't follow you.*
7 John: *"I can't make it" means I can't go. If you're not busy, you can have the tickets.*
8 Yoko: *Great! I haven't got any plans for tomorrow.*
9 John: *I've got the tickets in my pocket. Here you are.* [4]
10 Yoko: *Great! Thanks a lot.*
11 John: *That's okay.* [5] *By the way Yoko, have you got a Kleenex?*
12 Yoko: *A Kleenex? What does "a Kleenex" mean?*
13 John: *"A Kleenex" means a tissue.*
14 Yoko: *Sure. Here you are. Have you got a cold?*
15 John: *No. I've got a runny nose. Umm . . . er . . . Yoko?*
16 Yoko: *Yeah? What?*
17 John: *Have you got another pack? I haven't got any tissues, and this pack's nearly empty!*
18 Yoko: *Don't worry! I've got a new pack in my bag. Here you are.*
19 John: *Great! Thanks Yoko!*
20 Yoko: *No problem, John. Anyway, I gotta go now.* [6] *Thanks for the tickets!*
21 John: *That's okay. Have a nice time! See you later!*
22 Yoko: *Okay. Thanks again. See you round!*

THE JAPANESE STORY

6c
持っている

持っている - ジョンはヨーコに無料券をあげます。

1 ジョン: やあ、ヨーコ。レストランはどうだった？[1]

2 ヨーコ: とても楽しく食事できたわ。サイコーだったわよ。

3 ジョン: よかった。ところで、明日の夜何か予定ある？

4 ヨーコ: 明日の夜？　何もないけど、どうして？

5 ジョン: あのさ … 明日の夜の映画のタダ券を何枚か持ってるんだけど、[2] 忙しくて、できないんだよね …

6 ヨーコ: 「できない(I can't make it.)」ってどういう意味？[3] 私、分からないわ。

7 ジョン: 「できない」っていうのは「行けない」ってことだよ。もし君が忙しくないんだったら、券をあげるよ。（券を持っていってもいいよ。）

8 ヨーコ: うれしい！明日は何も予定がないのよ。

9 ジョン: ポケットの中に券があるんだ。ほら、どうぞ。[4]

10 ヨーコ: ほんとうにうれしいわ。ありがとう。

11 ジョン: どういたしまして。[5] ところでヨーコ、クリネックスはあるかな？

12 ヨーコ: クリネックス？「クリネックス」ってどういう意味？

13 ジョン: 「クリネックス」はティッシュのことさ。

14 ヨーコ: ええ、持ってるわ。はいどうぞ。風邪を引いたの？

15 ジョン: いや。鼻水が出るんだ。あ … あのさ … ヨーコ？

16 ヨーコ: ええ、何？

17 ジョン: もう一つある？　僕はティッシュを持ってないんだ。このパックはほとんど空だ。

18 ヨーコ: 心配しなくていいわよ！新しいパックを持ってるわ。バッグの中よ。どうぞ。

19 ジョン: やった！ヨーコ、ありがとう！

20 ヨーコ: どういたしまして、ジョン。私、もう行かなくちゃ。[6] 券をどうもありがとう。

21 ジョン: 構わないよ。楽しんでおいでね。また今度！

22 ヨーコ: オーケー。ほんとうにありがとね。またね！

6d
持っている

Simon Says - Easy Conversational English
EXAMPLES

A: What do you think of rugby?
B: Rugby? Oh, it's a great game.

* * *

A: How do you like living in Sapporo?
B: I love it, but the winters are cold.

* * *

A: Have you got any brothers, Michael?
B: Yeah. I've got four.

* * *

A: Have you got a pen?
B: Sure. Here you are.
A: Thanks a lot.
B: No problem.

* * *

A: You got any tissues?
B: Yeah. Here you go.
A: Thanks.
B: That's OK.

* * *

A: What does "selfie" mean?
B: "Selfie" means taking your own photo.

* * *

A: What do you mean by "YOLO"?
B: "YOLO" means You Only Live Once.

* * *

A: Do you have to leave now?
B: Yeah. I've gotta go home by ten.

A: ラグビーについてどう思いますか？
B: ラグビーですか？良いスポーツだね。

* * *

A: 札幌の生活はいかがでしょうか？
B: 大好きだけど、冬はやっぱり寒いですね。

* * *

A: マイケル、兄弟はいますか？
B: ええ。４人兄弟がいます。

５人兄弟です。

* * *

A: ペン、ありますか？
B: はい。どうぞ。
A: ありがとう。
B: どういたしまして。

* * *

A: ティッシュ持ってる？
B: ええ。はいどうぞ。
A: どうも。
B: どういたしまして。

* * *

A: 「selfie」ってどういう意味ですか？
B: 「selfie」というのは自撮りのことです。

* * *

A: さっき言った「YOLO」ってどういう意味？
B: 「YOLO」というのは人生一度きりです。

* * *

A: 今帰らないとだめですか？
B: うん。１０時までに帰らないと...

LEARN THESE SENTENCES

1 ...(について)どう思う？ What do you think of... ?

Look at the diagram. Do you understand?

How'd you like dogs?
I'm a cat person. Dogs are smelly!

標準日本語	標準英語	会話的
...について どう思う？	What do you think of/about ...	*What d'you think of ...?*
	How do you like ...	*How'd you like ...?*

日本語	会話的な英語
野球について どう思う？	*How'd you like baseball?*
彼の考え、どう思う？	*What d'you think of his idea?*
その本について どう思う？	*What d'you think about the book?*

What d'you think of beer?
I love beer! I'm crazy about it!

2 無料券持ってるよ。 I've got some free tickets.

Look at the diagram. Do you understand?

How many baseball caps have you got?
I've got lots of caps.

標準日本語	have/has	have --> have got
持ってる	I have ... She has ... Do you have ...? Does she have ...? I don't have ... She doesn't have ...	I have got ... She has got ... Have you got ...? Has she got ...? I haven't got ... She hasn't got ...
会話的な省略	I have got ... She has got ... Have you got ...? Has she got ...? I haven't got ... She hasn't got ...	I've got ... She's got ... (Have) you got ...? (Has) she got ...? I haven't got ... She hasn't got ...
例 1	新しい車があるから、お金がないの。	*I've got a new car, so I haven't got any money.*
例 2	彼女は短い髪してる。	*She's got short hair.*

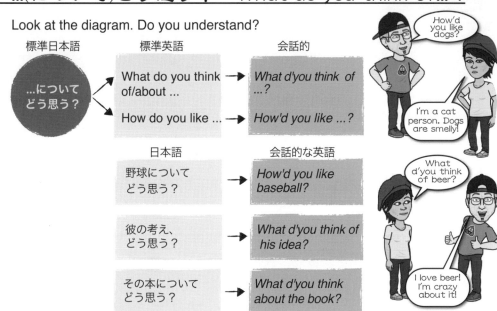

haveより、've gotの方が会話的だよ。

I've got a twin!
....?

LEARN THESE SENTENCES

Look at these questions. Do you understand?

口語に近いけど、質問の省略は会話的で言いやすいよ。

質問1	ペンがありますか?	→	*Have you got a pen?*
質問2	ペン、ありますか?	→	*You got a pen?*
質問3	ペン、ある?	→	*Got a pen?*

Got any money?

Nah.

Me neither!

You can use *have got* in many ways. Look at the examples.

| 色々 | 2匹の犬を飼っています。
ジェーンは脚が長い。
彼らには新車がある。
我々には時間がない。
彼は風邪を引いた。 | → | *I've got 2 dogs.*
Jane's got long legs.
They've got a new car.
We've got no time.
He's got a cold. |

You OK?

Nah. I've got a cold...

3　...どういう意味ですか？　What does ... mean?

Look at the diagram. Do you understand?

標準日本語	標準英語	会話的
...ってどういう意味ですか？	What does ... mean? →	What's ... mean?
	What do you mean by ...? →	What d'you mean by ...?

What does "ASAP" mean?

"ASAP" means "as soon as possible".

聞いた言葉が分からないとき、「What do you mean by ...?」を使おう。

	日本語	会話的な英語
例1	「LA」ってどういう意味ですか？	→ *What's "LA" mean?*
例2	さっき言った「selfie」（自撮り）ってどういう意味ですか？	→ *What d'you mean by " selfie"?*
例3	さっき言った「hangry」（空腹のイライラ感）ってどういう意味ですか？	→ *What d'ya mean by "hangry"?*

I'm hangry!

What do you mean by "hangry"?

Hangry means hungry & angry!

LEARN THESE SENTENCES

4　はい、どうぞ。 Here you are.

Give me a beer please! ♬
Sure. Here you are!

Look at the diagram. Do you understand?

標準日本語	標準英語	会話的
どうぞ →	Please. Here you are. →	*Here you go.* *Here you are.*

5　どういたしまして。 That's okay.

You're welcome より That's OK と No problem の方が会話的なので、どんどん使おう。

Please show me your smart phone.
OK. Here you go.
Thanks.
No problem.

Look at the diagram. Do you understand?

標準日本語	標準英語	会話的
どういたしまして →	You're welcome. Not at all. Don't mention it. →	*That's OK. (okay)* *No problem.*

	日本語	会話的な英語
例1	A: はい、どうぞ。 B: どうも。 A: どういたしまして。 →	A: *Here you are.* B: *Thanks.* A: *No problem.*
例2	A: どうぞ。 B: ありがとう。 A: いいえ。 →	A: *Here you are.* B: *Thanks a lot.* A: *That's OK.*

Thanks for the beer!
No problem.

6　行かなくちゃ。 I gotta go.

Look at the diagram. Do you understand?

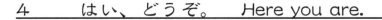

I got a drink と I gotta drink は似てない？よく読んでね。

Please pay!
I gotta go!

標準日本語	標準英語	会話的
行かなくちゃ	I must go. I have to go. I have got to go. →	*I must go.* *I hafta go.* *I've got to go.* *I've gotta go.* *I gotta go.*

Look at the diagram. Do you understand?

have (got)	飲み物を持っています。 飲み物を持っている。 飲み物、持ってる。 →	*I have a drink.* *I have got a drink.* *I've got a drink.*
vs		
have (got) to	飲まなければならない。 飲まないと… 飲まなくちゃ。 →	*I have to drink.* *I have got to drink.* *I've got to drink.* *I've gotta drink.*

CHALLENGE STAGE

Challenge 1. *Fill in the blanks from the list.*

1 Bart: I've got some free tickets for a concert tomorrow night but I'm tied up, so ...

2 Lisa: 「縛られてる、」ってどういう意味ですか? I don't understand.

3 Bart: I'm tied up means I'm very busy, so I can't go. Would you like the tickets?

4 Lisa: Yes please! 明日は何も予定がないんです。

5 Bart: I've got the tickets in my bag. どうぞ。

6 Lisa: Wonderful! Thanks very much.

7 Bart: いいえ、どういたしまして。 By the way Lisa, have you got a biro?

8 Lisa: A biro? 「バイロウ」ってどういう意味ですか？

9 Bart: A biro means a pen. I forgot my pencil case!

10 Lisa: Sure. どうぞ、バート。

11 Bart: Thanks. Um, Lisa, have you got a pad? I forgot to bring my notebook too.

12 Lisa: Don't worry! 使ってないノートを持っています。 Here you are.

13 Bart: Great! Thanks Lisa.

14 Lisa: That's okay. とにかく、もう行かなくちゃ。 Thanks for the tickets.

15 Bart: That's OK Lisa. Have a good time! See you later!

16 Lisa: Sure. Thanks again.

Choose the best sentence for the blanks:

a) No problem.
b) What does "a biro" mean?
c) I haven't got any plans for tomorrow.
d) What do you mean by "I'm tied up"?
e) Here you go, Bart.
f) I've got a spare notebook.
g) Anyway, I gotta go now.
h) Here you are.

CHALLENGE STAGE

Challenge 2. *Circle the correct answer.*

1. You ask your doctor their opinion(意見) about acupuncture (鍼).What do you say?
   (a) What do you think acupuncture? (b) What are you thinking acupuncture?
   (c) What are you think acupuncture? (d) What do you think of acupuncture?

2. You ask your friend how he feels about *karaoke*. What do you say?
   (a) How do you think *karaoke*? (b) How do you like *karaoke*?
   (c) How do you sing *karaoke*? (d) How do you know *karaoke*

3. Which sentence is the same as *I have a headache* (頭痛)?
   (a) I am a headache. (b) I have got to headache.
   (c) I got to headache. (d) I've got a headache.

4. Which sentence is NOT the same as *We do not have any time*?
   (a) We haven't got any time. (b) We've got no time.
   (c) We don't have any time. (d) We don't haven't got no time.

5. Which question is NOT the same as *Do you have a pen*?
   (a) You got a pen? (b) Have you got a pen?
   (c) Got a pen? (d) Do you got a pen?

6. The answer is; *VIP means Very Important Person*. What is the question?
   (a) What does VIP mean? (b) What does mean VIP?
   (c) VIP is mean what? (d) What mean is to VIP?

7. Your friend says *Please buy some SPAM.* You don't understand. What do you say?
   (a) What do you mean by SPAM? (b) What do you SPAM mean?
   (c) What SPAM are you? (d) What do SPAM is mean?

8. Your friend Michael gives you a basketball. What does he say? (はい、どうぞ。)
   (a) Here is it. (b) Here please.
   (c) Here you are. (d) Here are you.

9. Michael gives you a basketball. You say *Thank you.* Michael says, (どういたしまして。)
   (a) That's a problem. (b) That's okay.
   (c) That's not okay. (d) You're not welcome.

10. I must get up at 6 o'clock tomorrow. Which expression is NOT the same?
    (a) I have to get up at 6. (b) I have got to get up at 6.
    (c) I have got get up at 6. (d) I've gotta get up at 6.

CHALLENGE STAGE

Challenge 3. Did you read the English story?
Let's check!

1. What did Yoko think of the restaurant?
   (i) *She really enjoyed the food.*
   (ii) *She really enjoyed the music.*
   (iii) *She really enjoyed the mood.*
   (iv) *She really hated the food.*

2. Has Yoko got any plans for tomorrow night?
   (i) *Yes, she's busy.*
   (ii) *Yes, she's going swimming.*
   (iii) *Yes, she's meeting Paul.*
   (iv) *No, she hasn't got any plans.*

3. What does John give her?
   (i) *He gives her some money.*
   (ii) *He gives her some free tickets.*
   (iii) *He gives her some cigarettes.*
   (iv) *He doesn't give her anything.*

4. When is the movie?
   (i) *The movie is tonight.*
   (ii) *The movie is tomorrow night.*
   (iii) *The movie is next week.*
   (iv) *The movie is on Sunday.*

5. Why can't John go to the movies?
   (i) *He can't go because he's busy.*
   (ii) *He can't go because he has no money.*
   (iii) *He can't go because he hates movies.*
   (iv) *He doesn't want to go.*

6. What does "a Kleenex" mean?
   (i) *"A Kleenex" means a lighter.*
   (ii) *"A Kleenex" means a pen.*
   (iii) *"A Kleenex" means a tissue.*
   (iv) *"A Kleenex" means a cleaner.*

7. What does "I can't make it" mean?
   (i) *It means I can't cook.*
   (ii) *It means I can't sleep.*
   (iii) *It means I can't write very well.*
   (iv) *It means I can't go.*

8. Has John got a cold?
   (i) *No. He's got the flu.*
   (ii) *No. He's got an allergy.*
   (iii) *No. He's got a runny nose.*
   (iv) *No. He's got a headache.*

9. Where are Yoko's tissues?
   (i) *They are in her coat pocket.*
   (ii) *They are in her bag.*
   (iii) *They are in her hand.*
   (iv) *They are in her room.*

10. At the end, what does John say to Yoko?
   (i) *Have a nice time.*
   (ii) *Have a nice day.*
   (iii) *Have a nice trip.*
   (iv) *Have a nice meal.*

7a 好み

"Crazy about Eric."

QUICK START

好みじゃない	僕の好みの音楽ではない。	*It's not my sort of music.*	***...not my sort...***
	トムはタイプじゃない。	*Tom's not my type of guy.*	
	ビールは好みじゃない。	*Beer is not my kind of drink.*	
どんな	どんな音楽が好きですか。	*What type of music do you like.*	***What sort of***
	どんな映画でしたか？	*What sort of movie was it?*	
	どんなスポーツを見るの？	*What kind of sports do you watch?*	
好き嫌い	パスタが大好きです。	*I'm crazy about pasta.*	***love/hate***
	パスタは最高！	*Pasta is cool./Pasta rocks!*	
	貝類は大嫌い。	*I can't stand shellfish.*	
	貝類は最低！	*Shellfish sucks./I hate shellfish.*	
その他	....のことを聞いたことがない。	*Never heard of him/her/it.*	***Other***
	一番好きな...は何ですか？	*Who/What is your favorite . . .?*	

You got it? (分かった？)

☺

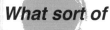

☹

- もう分かりましたか？
- チャレンジをやってみよう。
- *7f, 7g & 7h (ページ68~70)*をトライしよう。

- ***You got it?***
- ***Try the challenge section:***
- ***Exercises 7f, 7g, 7h (pages 68~70)***

- まだ分かりませんか？
- まず、*7b, 7c, 7d & 7e*を読んで*(ページ62~67)*
- *7f, 7g & 7h (ページ68~70)*をトライしよう。

- ***You don't get it? Not sure?***
- ***Read Sections 7b, 7c, 7d & 7e (pages 62~67)***
- ***Then, try exercises 7f, 7g, 7h (pages 68~70)***

THE ENGLISH STORY

Likes & dislikes - John and Yoko talk about movies and music.

1 John: *Hi Yoko. How was the movie?*

2 Yoko: *It was pretty good, but it wasn't my sort of movie.*[1]

3 John: *What was it called?*

4 Yoko: *It was called Rambo 17.*

5 John: *What sort of movie was it?*[2]

6 Yoko: *It was an action movie.*

7 John: *What sort of movie do you like?*

8 Yoko: *Well ... I guess I like comedies and romance movies. What about you, John? What type of movie do you like?*

9 John: *Hmm ... I like action movies and horror movies.*

10 Yoko: *Horror movies? Yuck! I can't stand horror movies.*[3]

11 John: *Yeah? What about music, Yoko? What kind of music do you like?*

12 Yoko: *Let me see ... I'm crazy about rock and heavy metal.*[4]

13 John: *Who's your favorite musician?*[5]

14 Yoko: *I really like Eric Clapton. He's a great guitarist.*

15 John: *Yeah. He's really good. What do you think of Jimi Hendrix?*

16 Yoko: *'Never heard of him!*[6] *Anyway John, what sort of music do you like?*

17 John: *I like '60s and '70s rock. You know, the Stones, the Doors, the Beatles ...*

18 Yoko: *The Beatles? 'Never heard of them!*

19 John: *You've never heard of the Beatles? Oh Yoko!*

20 Yoko: *Ha ha! Just joking! Of course I've heard of them!*

21 John: *Very funny Yoko!*

THE JAPANESE STORY

7c
好み

好み - ジョンはヨーコに好きな映画と音楽について話します。

1 ジョン: やあヨーコ。映画はどうだった？

2 ヨーコ: とてもよかったけど、私の趣味じゃなかったわ。[1]

3 ジョン: 何て映画だったの？

4 ヨーコ: 「ランボー１７」よ。

5 ジョン: どんな映画だった？[2]

6 ヨーコ: アクション映画よ。

7 ジョン: 君はどんな映画が好きなの？

8 ヨーコ: そうねえ ... コメディーや恋愛映画が好きだわ。ジョンはどうなの？ どんな映画が好き？

9 ジョン: そうだなあ... アクションやホラー映画が好きだよ。

10 ヨーコ: ホラー映画？ いやだわ！ 私、ホラー映画は大嫌いなの。[3]

11 ジョン: そうかい？ 音楽のほうはどうなんだい、ヨーコ？ どんな音楽が好きなの？

12 ヨーコ: えっとね ... ロックとヘビー・メタルが大好きよ。[4]

13 ジョン: いちばん好きなミュージシャンは誰？[5]

14 ヨーコ: エリック・クラプトンが大好きよ。すごいギタリストだわ。

15 ジョン: そうだね、彼はいいね。ジミー・ヘンドリクスはどう思う？

16 ヨーコ: 知らないわ。[6] とにかくジョン、 あなたはどんな音楽が好きなの？

17 ジョン: 僕は１９６０年代、７０年代のロックが好きだな。ほら、（ローリング・）ストーンズやドアーズやビートルズや...

18 ヨーコ: ビートルズですって？ 全然知らないわ！

19 ジョン: ビートルズを知らないの？ ああ、ヨーコったら！

20 ヨーコ: ふふふ！ 冗談よ。もちろん知ってるわよ。

21 ジョン: そう、おもしろいジョークだね、ヨーコ！

EXAMPLES

A: *Marilyn, what do you think of John?*
B: *Hmmm ... John's not my sort of guy.*

* * *

A: *I love winter. How about you?*
B: *Winter's not my type of season.*

* * *

A: *What sort of sports do you like?*
B: *I like boxing. How 'bout you?*
A: *Yeah - boxing is cool.*

* * *

A: *What kind of food do you like, Bart?*
B: *I'm crazy about pizza.*
A: *Yeah? What's your favorite pizza?*
B: *I really like Hawaiian.*

* * *

A: *What's your favorite movie, Roy?*
B: *I love "Jaws". How about you Peter?*
A: *Yeah, "Jaws" rocks.*

* * *

A: *What do you think of sushi?*
B: *Sushi? Yuck! I can't stand sushi!*

* * *

A: *How do you like rap music?*
B: *Rap? Rap sucks! I hate it.*

* * *

A: *Do you like Japanese enka?*
B: *Enka? No idea! Never heard of it.*

A: マリリン、ジョンについてどう思う？
B: そうね、タイプじゃないわ。

* * *

A: 冬好き！ 君はどう？
B: 冬はあまり好みじゃないですね。

* * *

A: どういうスポーツが好きですか？
B: ボクシングが好きだよ。あなたは？
A: うん。好きですね。

* * *

A: バートはどういう食べ物好きですか？
B: ピザが大好きですよ。
A: そう？ 一番好きなピザは何ですか？
B: ハワイアンがとても好きです。

* * *

A: ロイ、一番好きな映画は何ですか？
B: 「ジョーズ」が大好きです！
ピーターは？
A: うん。「ジョーズ」は最高！

* * *

A: 寿司についてどう思いますか？
B: 寿司？ マズイ！ 大嫌いです。

* * *

A: ラップミュージックについてどう思う？
B: ラップ？ 最低最悪！ 大嫌いです。

* * *

A: 日本の演歌が好きですか？
B: 演歌？ 知らん！ 聞いたことがない。

LEARN THESE SENTENCES

7e 好み

1 …は好みじゃないです … not my sort/kind/type of …

Look at the diagram. Do you understand?

Dogs are not my kind of pet.

日本語	形					会話的
…は好みじゃないです。 →	am		your	kind		→ …'s not my **sort** of …
			their			
	is	not	my	sort	of	…isn't her **type** of …
			her			
	are		his	type		…aren't our **kind** of …

kindとsortとtypeの意味は同じだよ。

日本語		会話的な英語
レゲエは好みじゃないです。	→	*Reggae's not my **sort** of music.*
マイケルは彼女のタイプではないです。	→	*Michael isn't her **type** of guy.*
犬は私達の好みじゃないですね。	→	*Dogs aren't our **kind** of pets.*

What d'you think of pizza?
Pizza's not my sort of food.

2 どんな…が…ですか？ What sort/kind/type of …

Look at the diagram. Do you understand?

標準日本語	どんな		どんな物
どんな… →	What **kind** of …	→	*What **kind** of food…*
	What **sort** of …	→	*What **sort** of music…*
	What **type** of …	→	*What **type** of sport…*

What kind of vegetables do you like?

	日本語		会話的な英語
例1	どんな映画でしたか？	→	*What kind of movie was it?*
例2	彼はどんな車を買ったの？	→	*What sort of car did he buy?*
例3	どのような仕事をしたいですか？	→	*What type of job do you want?*

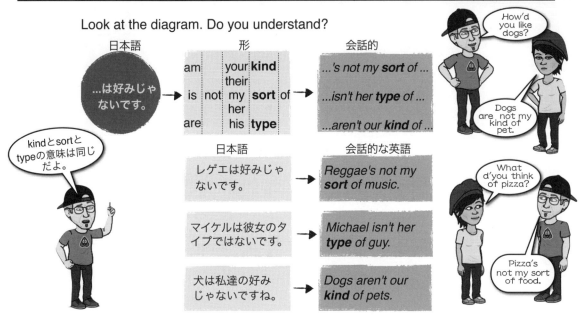

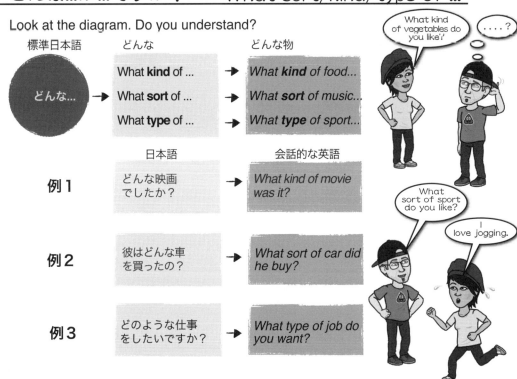

What sort of sport do you like?
I love jogging.

LEARN THESE SENTENCES

3 ... が大嫌いです。 I can't stand...

You wanna go to a disco?
No way! Discos suc

Look at the diagram. Do you understand?

標準日本語	標準英語		会話的
大嫌い...	I don't like ... I hate ... I dislike ...	→	*I can't stand...* *I hate ...* *...sucks.*

	日本語		会話的な英語
例 1	ブロッコリーが 大嫌いです。	→	*I can't stand broccoli.*
例 2	彼女は早起きが 大嫌いです。	→	*She hates getting up early.*
例 3	仕事は最低です！	→	*Work sucks!*
suck(s) (俗語)	学校嫌い！ 早起きはヤダ！ 車は大嫌い！ タバコは最低最悪だ！ オマエは嫌いだ！	→	*School sucks!* *Getting up early sucks!* *Cars suck!* *Cigarettes suck!* *You suck!*

Please wear a necktie tomorrow.
I can't stand wearing neckties.

Suckは短くて、使いやすいけど、**s**を付けるかどうか気をつけよう。

Did you catch a cold?
Yeah. This cold sucks!

4 ... が大好きです。 I'm crazy about ...

Look at the diagram. Do you understand?

標準日本語	標準英語		会話的
大好き	I like ... I love ... I adore ...	→	*I'm crazy about ...* *I love ...* *... is cool.* *... rocks.*

	日本語		会話的な英語
例 1	彼はサッカーに 夢中です。	→	*He's crazy about soccer.*
例 2	私は映画を観る のが大好きです。	→	*I love watching movies.*

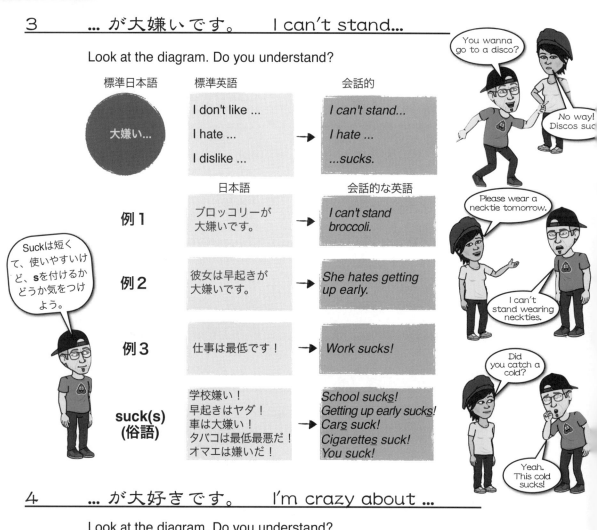

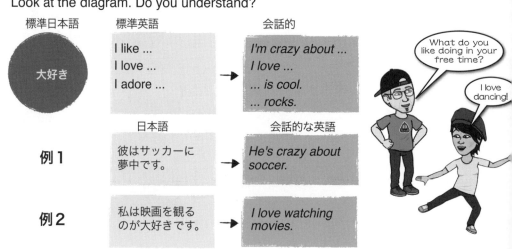

What do you like doing in your free time?
I love dancing!

sucksと同じように、rocksも俗語だよ。若い気持ちで使おう！

LEARN THESE SENTENCES

	日本語		会話的な英語
例3	犬はいいよ！	→	*Dogs are cool!*
例4	猫は最高！	→	*Cats rock!*
まあまあ	ウサギはまあまあです。	→	*Rabbits are OK.* *Rabbits are all right.* *Rabbits are average.*

What do you think about beer?
I'm crazy about beer!

好きでも、嫌いでも、まあまあでも、パターンは2つだけだよ。

形

パターン1 →	*I*	*love*	*cats.*
	I	*am crazy about*	*cats.*
	I	*hate*	*dogs.*
	I	*can't stand*	*dogs.*
パターン2 →	*Cats*	*are cool.*	
	Cats	*rock.*	
	Dogs	*suck*	
	Rabbits	*are OK.*	
	Rabbits	*are all right*	
	Rabbits	*are average.*	

Do you like cats?
Yeah. They are cool!
How 'bout dogs?
Hmm. Dogs are OK.

5　一番好きな…は？　Who's your favorite …?

Look at the diagram. Do you understand?

標準日本語		標準英語		会話的
一番好きな…	→	Who is your favorite ... ? What is your favorite ... ?	→	*Who's your favorite ... ?* *What's your favorite ... ?*

	日本語		会話的な英語
例	A: 一番好きな色は何ですか。 B: 黄色が好きです。	→	A: *What's your favorite color?* B: *I like yellow.*

What's your favorite
Beer rocks!

6　知らない。　Never heard of (him/it).

Look at the diagram. Do you understand?

標準日本語		標準英語		会話的
知らない (聞いたことがない。)	→	I have never heard of him. I have never heard of it.	→	*Never heard of 'im.* *Never heard of it.*

Do you know Furano?
Furano? Never heard of it.

CHALLENGE STAGE

Challenge 1. *Fill in the blanks from the list.*

1 Paul: Hi John. How was the book?

2 John: It was okay. でも私の好みの本ではありませんでした。

3 Paul: I see. 何という本でしたか？

4 John: It was called "Imagine".

5 Paul: どんな本でしたか？

6 John: It was a fantasy book.

7 Paul: ジョンはどんな本が好きですか？

8 John: Hmmm. I like love stories and adventure novels. What about you Paul?

どんな本が好きですか？

9 Paul: I like war stories and crime stories.

10 John: Crime stories! いや！ 犯罪の話は大嫌いだ。

11 Paul: Yeah? Too bad, John.

Choose the best sentence for the blanks:

a) What type of books do you like?
b) What was it called?
c) But it wasn't my type of book.
d) Yuck! I can't stand crime stories!
e) What sort of book was it?
f) What kind of books do you like, John?

CHALLENGE STAGE

Challenge 2. *Circle the correct answer.*

1. You like listening to jazz, but you don't like country. What can you say?
   (a) Country is not my sort of like. (b) Country is not my sort of music.
   (c) Country is not my like of music. (d) Country is not my sort like music.

2. Which expression (表現) is the SAME as *What kind of beer do you like?*
   (a) What size of beer do you like? (b) What sort of beer do you like?
   (c) What cost of beer do you like? (d) What color of beer do you like?

3. The answer is *I like dark, cold, rainy days.* What is the question?
   (a) What type of weather do you like? (b) What weather type is like you?
   (c) What is you like weather type? (d) What type of like do you weather?

4. Which question is bad?
   (a) What sort of food do you like? (b) What do you think of Japanese food?
   (c) What is your favorite food? (d) What do you like food type?

5. If you really like Chinese cooking, what can you say?
   (a) I'm crazy about Chinese cooking. (b) I can't stand Chinese cooking.
   (c) I really hate Chinese cooking. (d) Chinese cooking is all right.

6. The expression (表現) *I really like dancing* is the same as:
   (a) Dancing sucks. (b) Dancing is average.
   (c) I dislike dancing. (d) Dancing is cool.

7. The expression (表現) *I hate walking* is the same as:
   (a) Walking can't stand. (b) Walking is crazy about.
   (c) Walking sucks. (d) Walking is all right.

8. You don't like soccer, but you don't hate soccer (サッカーはまあまあです。). You can say:
   (a) Soccer is cool. (b) Soccer is OK.
   (c) Soccer is like. (d) Soccer is dislike.

9. Your friend says *Do you like parkour?* (パルクール) You don't know parkour, so what do you say?
   (a) Never heard of it. (b) Never heard to it.
   (c) Never heard it. (d) Never heard by it.

10. Which three words are the same?
   (a) [kind, sort, type] (b) [kind, sort, like]
   (c) [sort, kind, suit] (d) [type, sort, favorite]

CHALLENGE STAGE

Challenge 3. Did you read the English story?
Let's check!

1. How was the movie?
   - *(i) It was pretty good and Yoko liked it.*
   - *(ii) It was pretty bad and Yoko didn't like it.*
   - *(iii) It was pretty good but Yoko didn't like it.*
   - *(iv) It was pretty bad but Yoko liked it.*

2. What was the movie called?
   - *(i) It was called Rocky 17.*
   - *(ii) It was called Rambo 17.*
   - *(iii) It was called Rocky 70.*
   - *(iv) It was called Rambo 70.*

3. What sort of movie was it?
   - *(i) It was a comedy.*
   - *(ii) It was a horror movie.*
   - *(iii) It was a romance movie.*
   - *(iv) It was an action movie.*

4. What kind of movie does Yoko like?
   - *(i) She likes comedies and romance movies.*
   - *(ii) She likes action and horror movies.*
   - *(iii) She likes musicals.*
   - *(iv) She likes adventure movies.*

5. What type of movie does John like?
   - *(i) He likes comedies and romance movies.*
   - *(ii) He likes science fiction movies.*
   - *(iii) He likes documentaries.*
   - *(iv) He likes action and horror movies.*

6. What kind of music does Yoko like?
   - *(i) She likes rock and heavy metal.*
   - *(ii) She likes classical music.*
   - *(iii) She likes rock and roll.*
   - *(iv) She likes punk rock.*

7. Who is Yoko's favorite musician?
   - *(i) Her favorite musician is Eric Clapton.*
   - *(ii) Her favorite musician is The Beatles.*
   - *(iii) Her favorite musician is Jimi Hendrix.*
   - *(iv) Her favorite musician is Rambo.*

8. Who has Yoko never heard of?
   - *(i) She's never heard of The Beatles.*
   - *(ii) She's never heard of Jimi Hendrix.*
   - *(iii) She's never heard of Eric Clapton.*
   - *(iv) She's never heard of The Eagles.*

9. What kind of music does John like?
   - *(i) He likes '80s and '90s rock.*
   - *(ii) He likes '70s and '80s rock.*
   - *(iii) He likes '60s and '70s rock.*
   - *(iv) He likes '50s and '60s rock.*

10. What bands does John like?
    - *(i) He likes the Stones, Doors and Beatles.*
    - *(ii) He likes the Rocks, Doors and Bugs.*
    - *(iii) He likes the Stones, Windows and Beatles.*
    - *(iv) He likes the Rocks, Windows and Bugs.*

"Is John there?"

QUICK START

いますか?

... さんと話したいのですが。	May/Can/Could I speak to ... ?
	Is ... in/there?
... さんはいますか?	I'd like to speak to ...

Hello

私ですが

私ですが。	Speaking.
	This is . . .

Speaking

電話する

彼に電話してごらん。	Call him. Ring him.
	Give him a call. Give him a ring.
	Call him. Telephone him.

Call

その他

間違い電話です。	You (must) have the wrong number.
ご用件は?	May/Can I help you?
席を外しています。	He's not in.

Other

You got it? (分かった?)

 ☺

 ☹

・もう分かりましたか?
・チャレンジをやってみよう。
・*8f, 8g & 8h (ページ78~80)をトライしよう。*

・まだ分かりませんか?
・まず、*8b, 8c, 8d & 8e*を読んで(ページ72~77)
・*8f, 8g & 8h (ページ78~80)をトライしよう。*

・*You got it?*
・*Try the challenge section:*
・*Exercises 8f, 8g, 8h (pages 78~80)*

・*You don't get it? Not sure?*
・*Read Sections 8b, 8c, 8d & 8e (pages 72~77)*
・*Then, try exercises 8f, 8g, 8h (pages 78~80)*

THE ENGLISH STORY

Telephones - Yoko makes three phone calls.

1 Voice: *Hello?*

2 Yoko: *Hello. Can I speak to John please?*[1]

3 Voice: *John? There's no John here. You must have the wrong number.*[2]

4 Yoko: *Oh! I'm sorry. Bye.*

5 Voice: *No problem. Good bye.*

~ ~

6 John: *Hello?*

7 Yoko: *Hello. Could I speak to John please?*

8 John: *Speaking ...*[3]

9 Yoko: *John! It's me, Yoko!*

10 John: *Oh! Hi Yoko. How's it going?*

11 Yoko: *Not too good. I feel sick and I threw up this morning.*

12 John: *Hmm ... That sounds bad, Yoko. You'd better go to the doctor.*

13 Yoko: *But I don't know any doctors here.*

14 John: *That's okay. Here's my doctor's number. Give him a call.*[4] *The number is 385-4411.*

15 Yoko: *Okay, I'll call him now. G'bye. And thanks, John.*

16 John: *That's okay, Yoko. Call him now, and take care. Bye.*

~ ~

17 Clinic: *Good morning. Dr Feelgood's office. Can I help you?*[5]

18 Yoko: *Ah ... Yes please. I'd like to make an appointment to see the doctor.*

19 Clinic: *Certainly. Your name, madam?*

20 Yoko: *Sono. S-O-N-O.*

21 Clinic: *Is that your first name or last name?*

22 Yoko: *It's my surname.*

23 Clinic: *Okay, Ms Sono. The doctor can see you at three thirty.*

24 Yoko: *Great. Thanks very much. Goodbye.*

25 Clinic: *Goodbye.*

THE JAPANESE STORY

8c
電話

電話 - ヨーコは三回電話をかけます。

1 相手: もしもし?

2 ヨーコ: もしもし、ジョンと話したいのですが。[1]

3 相手: ジョン？ ジョンなんて奴はここにはいないよ。間違い電話じゃないのかい？[2]

4 ヨーコ: あら、ごめんなさい。さようなら。

5 相手: 構わないよ。さよなら。

～ ～

6 ジョン: もしもし？

7 ヨーコ: もしもし、ジョンと話したいのですが。

8 ジョン: 僕だけど…[3]

9 ヨーコ: ジョンね！　私よ、ヨーコよ！

10 ジョン: ああ、やあヨーコ！　調子はどうだい？

11 ヨーコ: それが、あまりよくないのよ。吐き気がして、今朝は戻しちゃったの。

12 ジョン: うーん… 調子悪そうだねえ、ヨーコ。病院に行った方がいいよ。

13 ヨーコ: でもここでは病院（直訳は「医者」）を知らないのよ。

14 ジョン: 大丈夫さ。僕の医者の電話番号を教えるよ。彼に電話してごらん。[4]

ヨーコ: 番号は385-4411だよ。

15 ジョン: オーケー、すぐに電話するわ。さよなら。あ、どうもありがとう、ジョン。

16 ヨーコ: どういたしまして、ヨーコ。すぐに電話するんだよ。お大事にね。バーイ。

～ ～

17 病院: おはようございます。フィールグッド先生のオフィスです。ご用件は？[5]

18 ヨーコ: あの… 先生に診察の予約をしたいのですが。

19 病院: かしこまりました。お名前は？

20 ヨーコ: ソノです。S-O-N-O。

21 病院: それはお名前でしょうか、名字でしょうか？

22 ヨーコ: 名字です。

23 病院: かしこまりました、ソノ様。先生との予約は３時半です。

24 ヨーコ: よかった。ありがとうございます。さようなら。

25 病院: 失礼します。

EXAMPLES

A: Hi. <u>Can I speak to</u> Ray please?

B: <u>This is</u> Ray.

*   *   *

A: Hello. <u>Could I speak to</u> Ron?

B: <u>Speaking</u> ...

*   *   *

A: Hello. <u>May I speak to</u> Bill, please?

B: Bill? <u>There's nobody called Bill here.</u> You must have <u>the wrong number.</u>

A: Oh! Sorry. Goodbye.

*   *   *

A: I'm busy now, so <u>call me</u> tomorrow.

B: OK. I'll <u>ring you</u> tomorrow.

A: <u>Phone me</u> in the morning, OK?

B: Sure. I'll <u>give you a call</u> at eleven.

*   *   *

A: Hello. Burton Snowboards. <u>May I help you?</u>

B: <u>I'd like to speak to</u> Mr. Burton.

*   *   *

A: Good morning. <u>Is Lisa there please?</u>

B: <u>She's out now. Please call back later.</u>

*   *   *

A: Hello. <u>Can I speak to</u> God?

B: <u>He's not in right now.</u> <u>Can I take a message?</u>

A: No. It's okay, thanks.

B: Alright. G'bye.

A: こんにちは。レイさんは<u>いますか？</u>

B: はい、<u>私</u>です。

*   *   *

A: こんにちは。ロンさんは<u>いますか？</u>

B: はい、<u>私</u>です。

*   *   *

A: こんにちは。ビルさんを<u>お願いします。</u>

B: ビルですか？ <u>ビルという人は、ここにい</u> <u>ませんよ。間違い電話</u>じゃないですか？

A: あららら。ごめん、さよなら。

*   *   *

A: 今忙しいから、明日電話してください。

B: 了解。明日、<u>電話します。</u>

A: 午前中に電話してね。

B: いいよ。１１時に<u>電話します。</u>

*   *   *

A: こんにちは。バートン・スノーボードです。 <u>ご用件は？</u>

B: バートンさんと<u>話したいんですけれど。</u>

*   *   *

A: おはようございます。リサさん、<u>いますか？</u>

B: <u>今いません。後でかけ直してください。</u>

*   *   *

A: こんにちは。神様と<u>話したいんですが。</u>

B: <u>神様は、今いません。</u> <u>伝言はありますか？</u>

A: いや、結構です。

B: わかりました。さようなら。

伝言は英語でmessageだよ。

LEARN THESE SENTENCES

1　...さんと話したいのですが。　Can I speak to ...?

Look at the diagram. Do you understand?

標準日本語	標準英語	会話的
...いますか？ →	May / Can I speak to ...? / Could Is ... in? Is ... there? I'd like to speak to ... →	same

Hello, Can I speak to Jack?

日本語	会話的な英語
ジョンさんと話したいんですが。 →	*I'd like to speak to John, please.*
太郎さん、いますか？ →	*Is Taro in?*
こんにちは。はるかさんをお願いします。 →	*May I speak to Haruka?*

Hi !
Is Peter in?

2　間違い電話...　Wrong number...

Look at the diagram. Do you understand?

標準日本語	標準英語	会話的
間違い電話... →	You (must) have (dialed) the wrong number. →	*Wrong number!*

Hi. Can I speak to Mike?
Mike? You must have the wrong number. There's no Mike here.

普段は、You have the wrong number が一番使いやすいよ。

	日本語	会話的な英語
丁寧	電話番号をお間違えではないでしょうか。 →	*You must have dialed the wrong number.*
普通	間違い電話ではないでしょうか。 →	*You have the wrong number.*
短い	間違い電話です。 →	*Wrong number!*

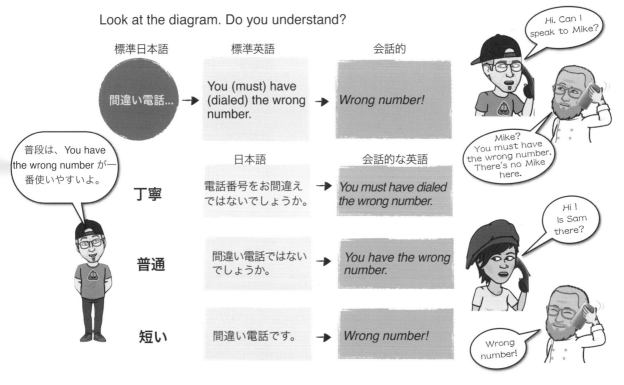

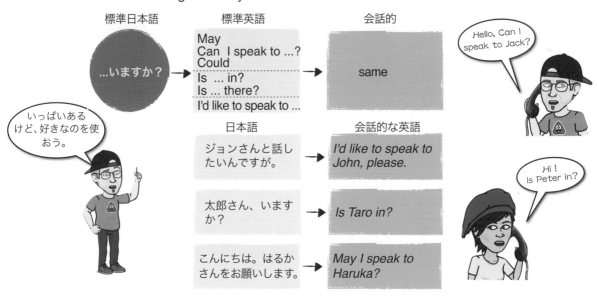

Hi !
Is Sam there?

Wrong number!

LEARN THESE SENTENCES

3 　　私ですが... 　　Speaking...

Look at the diagram. Do you understand?

標準日本語	標準英語	会話的
私ですが...	This is ... (name) This is he/she. Speaking.	*This is ... (name)* *Speaking.*

"I am John" と言わないで。一番楽なのは "Speaking".

Hello. I'd like to speak to John please.

	日本語	会話的な英語
例1	A: ジョン、いますか？ B: 僕ですけど...	A: *Is John there?* B: *Speaking...*
例2	A: ジム、お願いします。 B: はい。私ですが...	A: *May I speak to Jim?* B: *This is Jim.*

This is John.

4 　　彼に電話してごらん。 　　Give him a call.

Look at the diagram. Do you understand?

標準日本語	標準英語	例
電話する	call ring phone telephone give a call give a ring	***Ted called Bill.*** Ted **rang** Bill. Ted **phoned** Bill. Ted **telephoned** Bill. Ted **gave** Bill **a call**. Ted **gave** Bill **a ring**.

電話の「電話する」という言い方は、少なくとも6つだよ。

Can I call you tonight?

Sure. Ring me after 6.

	日本語	会話的な英語
例1	今晩は電話しないでね。	*Don't call me tonight!*
例2	来週電話してください。	*Please give me a call next week.*
例3	あとで電話しますから。	*I'll phone you later.*
例4	なんで電話してくれなかったの？	*Why didn't you ring me?*

What's wrong?

I lost my friend's number so I can't call her.

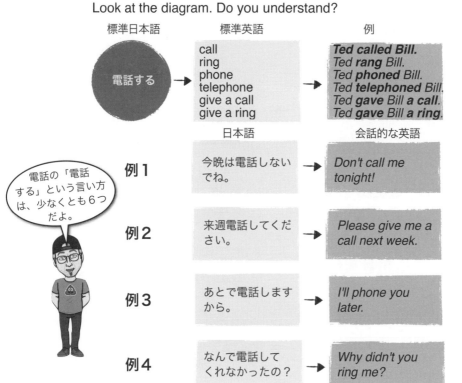

LEARN THESE SENTENCES

5　ご用件は？　Can I help you?

Look at the diagram. Do you understand?

全部よく使われているけど、May I help you とCan I help you? が一番使われているよ。

標準日本語		標準英語		会話的
ご用件は？	→	May I help you? Can I help you? How can I help you? How may I help you? What can I help you with?	→	*May I help you?* *Can I help you?* (よく使われている)

Hi.
Charlie's restaurant.
Can I help you?

	日本語		会話的な英語
例1	おはようございます。 小池靴履物店です。 ご用件は？	→	*Good morning.* *Koike's Shoe Shop.* ***May I help you?***
例2	こんにちは。 北海道警察です。 ご用件は？	→	*Good afternoon.* *Hokkaido Police.* ***How may I help you?***
例3	こんにちは。 ホテル・マヌです。 ご用件は？	→	*Hello.* *Hotel Manu.* ***Can I help you?***

Hello.
Three Johns Company.
Can we help you?

Hi !!
Yoko's Dance School.
May I help you?

6　今いません。　He's not in now.

Look at the diagram. Do you understand?

標準日本語		標準英語		会話的
席を外している。	→	... is not in. ... is out. ... is not here. ... has stepped out.	→	...'s not in (now). ...'s out (now). ...'s not here (now). ...'s stepped out.

Now(今)か right now(ただ今)を付けてもいいよ。例えば、He's out right now.

	日本語		会話的な英語
例1	A: ジョン、いますか？ B: ただ今、ジョンは席を外しています。	→	A: *Hi. Is John there?* B: *John's not in right now.*
例2	A: ジョン、いますか？ B: ただ今、ジョンは席を外しています。伝言はありますか。 A: ポールに電話をしてと伝えてください。 B: はい、分かりました。	→	A: *Hi. Is John there?* B: *John's not in right now. Can I take a message?* A: *Yes. Please tell him to call Paul.* A: *Sure. No problem.*

Hello. Could I speak to Paul please?
Sorry. He's out. Can I take a
Yes please. Tell him to call Yoko.
OK. Bye.

8f
電話

CHALLENGE STAGE

Challenge 1. *Fill in the blanks from the list.*

1 Voice: Hello?

2 Jane: Hello. ターザンをお願いします。

3 Voice: Tarzan? There's no Tarzan here. 間違い電話じゃないかい。

4 Jane: Oh. ごめんなさい. さようなら。

5 *(Jane tries to call Tarzan again.)*

6 Tarzan: Hello?

7 Jane: Hello. Can I speak to Tarzan please?

8 Tarzan: 私ですが... (ターザンです。)

9 Jane: Tarzan! It's me, Jane!

10 Tarzan: Oh. Hi Jane! How's it going?

11 Jane: あまり良くないわ。 I threw up this morning. I feel really sick.

12 Tarzan: Hmm. . . That sounds bad. You'd better go to the witch doctor!

13 Jane: でも、ここの魔法使いをひとりも知らないの。

14 Tarzan: That's okay. Here's my witch doctor's number. Give him a call!
The number is 666-6969.

15 Jane: わかった。すぐに電話するわ。 Bye. And thanks, Tarzan.

16 *(Jane calls the witch doctor.)*

17 Clinic: Good morning. Dr Mandela's Clinic. ご用件は？

18 Jane: I'd like to make an appointment to see the witch doctor please.

Choose the best sentence for the blanks:

a) Can I help you?
b) Not so good.
c) May I speak to Tarzan please?
d) You must have the wrong number.
e) This is Tarzan.
f) I'm sorry. Bye.
g) Okay. I'll call him now.
h) But I don't know any witch doctors here.

CHALLENGE STAGE

Challenge 2. *Circle the correct answer.*

1. You call your teacher. Somebody answers the phone. What do you say?
   (a) I'd like to speak for Simon, please. (b) I'd like to speak at Simon, please.
   (c) I'd like to speak by Simon, please. (d) I'd like to speak to Simon, please.

2. You want to talk with John. You call him. Which expression is NOT good?
   (a) May I speak to John, please? (b) Can I speak to John, please?
   (c) Is John in? (d) Does John there?

3. Your name is Bill. A guy calls you. He says *Could I speak to Bill?* What do you say?
   (a) This is Bill. (b) I am me.
   (c) Me Bill. (d) Bill is speaking.

4. Somebody calls you. It is a *wrong number*. Which expression is NOT good?
   (a) This is wrong. (b) You have the wrong number.
   (c) Wrong number. (d) You have dialed the wrong number.

5. You work part-time at NHK. There is a telephone call. You answer it. What do you say?
   (a) Hello. NHK. Can I help it? (b) Hello. NHK. Can you help me?
   (c) Hello. NHK. Can I help you? (d) Hello. NHK. Can it be helped?

6. Which expression is NOT similar to *How can I help you* (ご用件は)?
   (a) How may I help you? (b) May I help you?
   (c) Can I help you? (d) How can you help me?

7. Your friend says to you *I called twice this morning*. Which expression is NOT the same?
   (a) I rang twice this morning. (b) I telephoned twice this morning.
   (c) I phoned twice this morning. (d) I teled twice this morning.

8. Your friend says *Give me a ring on Friday*. Which expression is the same?
   (a) Give me a tel on Friday. (b) Give me a rang on Friday.
   (c) Give me phoning on Friday. (d) Call me on Friday.

9. You telephone your teacher. The teacher is not at school. School reception says;
   (a) Sorry, but he's not out now. (b) Sorry, but he's not in now.
   (c) Sorry, but he's not right now. (d) Sorry, but he's stepped up now.

10. Your teacher is not at school. School reception asks if you have a message (伝言). He says:
   (a) Can you take a message? (b) Can I message you?
   (c) Can I take a message? (d) Do you want a massage?

CHALLENGE STAGE

Challenge 3. Did you read the English story?
Let's check!

1. Who does Yoko want to speak to?
   (i) She wants to speak to Paul.
   (ii) She wants to speak to John.
   (iii) She wants to speak to her mother.
   (iv) She doesn't want to speak to anybody.

2. Who does Yoko call at first?
   (i) She calls the clinic.
   (ii) She calls Paul.
   (iii) She calls a wrong number.
   (iv) She doesn't call anybody.

3. How is Yoko feeling ?
   (i) She's feeling great.
   (ii) She's feeling lonely.
   (iii) She's feeling excited.
   (iv) She isn't feeling too good.

4. What did Yoko do this morning?
   (i) She went shopping.
   (ii) She drank beer.
   (iii) She watched a movie.
   (iv) She threw up.

5. What is John's doctor's name?
   (i) His name is Doctor John.
   (ii) His name is Doctor Feelgood.
   (iii) His name is Doctor Sono.
   (iv) We don't know his name.

6. What is John's doctor's number?
   (i) His number is 385-4411.
   (ii) His number is 384-5511.
   (iii) His number is 385-1144.
   (iv) His number is 384-1155.

7. What does Yoko want to make?
   (i) She wants to make an appointment.
   (ii) She wants to make a life plan.
   (iii) She wants to make a cake.
   (iv) She wants to make a happy life.

8. What time does Yoko have to see the doctor?
   (i) She has to see the doctor at 3 o'clock.
   (ii) She has to see the doctor at 3:30.
   (iii) She has to see the doctor at 4 o'clock.
   (iv) She has to see the doctor at 4:30.

9. How many phone calls does Yoko make?
   (i) She makes one phone call.
   (ii) She makes two phone calls.
   (iii) She makes three phone calls.
   (iv) She makes four phone calls.

10. What does the receptionist say?
    (i) He says "May I help you?".
    (ii) He says "Can I help you?".
    (iii) He says "Do I help you?".
    (iv) He says "Will I help you?".

"What's wrong with me?"

どうしましたか？

頭が痛いです。

What seems to be the problem?

I've got a bad headache.

QUICK START

どうした？

どうしましたか？	What seems to be the problem?
どうしたの？	What's wrong? What's up?
〃 〃	What's the matter/problem? etc

What's wrong?

症状

熱がありますか？	Have you got a temperature?
腹痛がひどいんです。	I've got a bad stomach ache.
下痢をしていません。	I haven't got diarrhea.
二日酔いなんだ。	You've got a hangover.

...have got...

薬

毎食後3錠を飲んで。	Take 3 tablets after each meal.
食前に2錠を飲んで。	Take 2 tablets before meals.
食間に1錠を飲んで。	Take a tablet between meals.
4時間毎に、1錠を飲んで。	Take a pill every 4 hours.

Take 3 tablets

その他

どちら様でしょうか...	And you are ...
予約しています...	I have an appointment ...
回復した。	I'm better!

Other

You got it? (分かった？)

☺ ☹

・もう分かりましたか？
・チャレンジをやってみよう。
・9f, 9g & 9h (ページ88~90)をトライしよう。

・You got it?
・Try the challenge section:
・Exercises 9f, 9g, 9h (pages 88~90)

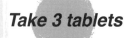

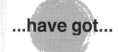

・まだ分かりませんか？
・まず、9b, 9c, 9d & 9eを読んで(ページ82~87)
・9f, 9g & 9h (ページ88~90)をトライしよう。

・You don't get it? Not sure?
・Read Sections 9b, 9c, 9d & 9e (pages 82~87)
・Then, try exercises 9f, 9g, 9h (pages 88~90)

THE ENGLISH STORY

Sick - Yoko goes to see the doctor.

1 Yoko: Hello. Doctor Feelgood?

2 Dr: Yes. And you are ... ? [1]

3 Yoko: Sono. Yoko Sono. I have an appointment [2] to see you at 3:30.

4 Dr: Well, it's 3:30 now, so come into my office.

5 (Yoko and Dr Feelgood go into Dr Feelgood's office.)

6 Dr: So, what seems to be the problem, [3] Ms Sono.

7 Yoko: Well, when I woke up this morning I felt sick. I had a stomachache and I threw up twice.

8 Dr: I see. Have you still got a stomachache? [4]

9 Yoko: Yes, a little bit. And I've got a slight headache, too.

10 Dr: Hm. I'll take your temperature and blood pressure.

11 Yoko: Okay.

12 (The doctor takes her temperature and blood pressure.)

13 Dr: Hmm. 37.3 degrees! You've got a temperature. You've also got high blood pressure. Did you have diarrhea last night or this morning?

14 Yoko: I don't follow you. What do you mean by "diarrhea"?

15 Dr: Diarrhea means ... Ah ... Did you go to the toilet many times?

16 Yoko: Oh! I see! I haven't got diarrhea, Dr Feelgood.

17 Dr: Okay. Did you drink anything last night, Ms Sono?

18 Yoko: Well. I had 3 or 4 drinks; some wine, beer and whisky I think. What's wrong with me, Doctor? Is it serious?

19 Dr: Well Ms Sono. It's not serious. I'll give you some medicine.

20 Yoko: Thanks Dr Feelgood, but what's the problem? What's wrong with me?

21 Dr: Ms Sono. You drank too much. You've got a bad hangover. That's all. Here's the medicine. Take 2 tablets after each meal. [5] Go home and rest.

THE JAPANESE STORY

9c
病気

病気 - ヨーコは病院に行きます。

1 ヨーコ: あの ...フィールグッド先生ですか？

2 医者: そうですが、あなたは ...？[1]

3 ヨーコ: ソノです。ソノ・ヨーコ。３時半に診察の予約をしています。[2]

4 医者: そうですか、今３時半ですね。診察室にお入りください。

5 （ヨーコとフィールグッド医師はフィールグッド医師の診察室に入る。）

6 医者: それで、ソノさん、どうしましたか？[3]

7 ヨーコ: あの ... 今朝起きたら吐き気がしました。 お腹が痛かったです。そして二回戻しました。

8 医者: わかりました。まだお腹が痛いですか？[4]

9 ヨーコ: ええ、少し。軽く頭痛もします。

10 医者: そうですね ... ちょっと、熱と血圧を計りましょうか。

11 ヨーコ: はい。

12 （お医者さんがヨーコさんの熱と血圧を計ります。）

13 医者: うーん、３７度３分ですね。熱がありますよ。 血圧も高いです。夕べか今朝、 下痢（diarrhea）をしましたか？

14 ヨーコ: 意味がわかりません。「下痢（diarrhea）」ってどういう意味ですか？

15 医者: 下痢（diarrhea）とは ... その ... トイレに何度も行きましたか？

16 ヨーコ: ああ、わかりました！　フィールグッド先生、下痢はしていません。

17 医者: わかりました。ソノさん、夕べ何か飲みましたか？

18 ヨーコ: ええと、３杯か４杯飲みました。ワインとビールとウィスキーだったと思います。先生、どこが悪いんですか？　重いのですか？

19 医者: いいですか、ソノさん。重くありませんよ。少し薬を出しましょう。

20 ヨーコ: ありがとう、先生。でも何が問題なんですか？　どこが悪いんですか？

21 医者: ソノさん、飲みすぎですよ。ひどい二日酔いなんですよ。それだけです。これが薬です。 毎食後錠剤を一錠飲みなさい。[5] 家に帰って休みなさい。

9d
病気

A: Hello. Doctor Spock?
B: Yes. And you are... ?
A: Kirk. James T. Kirk.

* * *

A: Good morning, Mr. Stanley.
B: Good morning. Ah... I don't think we've met.
A: My name is Livingstone.

* * *

A: Hi. Can I make an appointment to see the doctor?
B: Sure. The doctor can see you at 2 tomorrow.

* * *

A: What's the problem, Jack?
B: I've got a headache, Jill.

* * *

A: What's the trouble, Anne?
B: I've got a sore neck, Henry.

* * *

A: What's wrong with Shinzo?
B: Oh, he's got a bad heart.

* * *

A: You've still got a slight fever.
B: Yeah. I had a bad cold last week.

* * *

A: You've got a bad cold. I'll give you some medicine. Take two tablets after each meal.
B: Thanks, doctor.

A: こんにちは。スポック先生ですか？
B: はい。えー… あなたは…？
A: カークです。ジェームズ・T・カーク。

* * *

A: おはようございます、スタンレーさん。
B: おはようございます。あの、お会いしたことはないと思うんですが。
A: 私の名前はリビングストンです。

* * *

A: こんにちは。 先生に診察の予約をしたいのですが。
B: 分かりました。先生は明日の２時が空いています。

* * *

A: ジャック、どうしたの？
B: 頭が痛いんです、ジル。

* * *

A: アン、どうしたの？
B: 首が痛いんですよ、ヘンリー。

* * *

A: シンゾウはどうしたの？
B: なんか、彼は心臓が悪いんです。

* * *

A: まだ微熱があるんですね。
B: うん。先週ひどい風邪を引いたんだ。

* * *

A: あなたはひどい風邪にかかってるんですよ。薬をさしあげます。 毎食後、錠剤を２錠飲んでください。
B: はい、ありがとうございます、先生。

LEARN THESE SENTENCES

1　あなたは...?　And you are ...?

Look at the diagram. Do you understand?

日本語	標準英語	会話的
あなたは...? →	Who are you? →	*And you are ...* *I don't think we've met.* *I'm not sure we've met.* *Do I know you?*

	日本語	会話的な英語
普通 **(ちょっと堅い？)**	あなたは...? →	*And you are ...?*
丁寧	以前お会いしたことがないと思いますが... →	*I don't think we've met before.*
丁寧	会ったことがない気がしますが... →	*I'm not sure we've met.*
フレンドリー **(ちょっと面白い)**	僕は、君のことを知ってるかなあ... →	*Do I know you?*

2　予約をしている。　I have an appointment ...

Look at the diagram. Do you understand?

標準日本語	英語	違いは？
予約する	make an appointment →	プロフェッショナル
	make a reservation book (make a booking) →	サービス業

	日本語	会話的な英語
例 1	金曜日の４時に歯医者に診察の予約をしています。 →	*I have an appointment to see the dentist at 4PM on Friday.*
例 2	ご予約なさっていますか？ →	*Do you have an appointment?*
例 3	私は今日、医者に診てもらう予約がありました。 →	*I had a doctor's appointment today.*

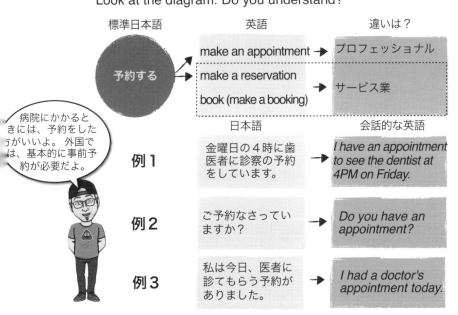

LEARN THESE SENTENCES

3　どうしましたか？　What seems to be the problem?

Look at the diagram. Do you understand?

日本語	いっぱい		会話的
どうしたの？	What's up? What's wrong? What's happened? What's the matter? What's the trouble? What's the problem?	→	*What's up?*

What's the matter?
I lost my smartphone.

一番無難なのは What's up? 挨拶にも使えるし...

	日本語		会話的な英語
丁寧	どうしましたか？	→	*What seems to be the problem?*
残念なとき	どうしたの？	→	*What's wrong?* *What's the problem?* *What's the trouble?* *What's the matter?*
一般	どうしたの？	→	*What's up?* *(What's happened?)*

What's up, John?
I have a date tonight!

4　...かかっている（症状）　... have got ...

Look at the diagram. Do you understand?

病気のこと、身体のこと、健康のことについて話をする時の動詞は have だよ。会話では、have より have got を使おう。
もう一度 Chapter 6 (have) を見てね。

標準日本語		使える場合が多い		会話的 (have got)
...かかっている。	→	風邪 熱 二日酔い 癌 下痢 頭痛 等	→	*Yoko's got a cold.* *She's got a fever.* *I've got a hangover.* *He hasn't got cancer.* *Don's got diarrhea.* *May's got a headache.*

What's wrong?
I've got a cold.

	日本語		会話的な英語
例1	お腹が痛いですか？	→	*Have you got a stomachache?*
例2	君、熱がないので、学校に行ってください。	→	*You haven't got a temperature, so please go to school!*
例3	インフルエンザにかかってるので、仕事を休む。	→	*I can't go to work because I've got the 'flu.*

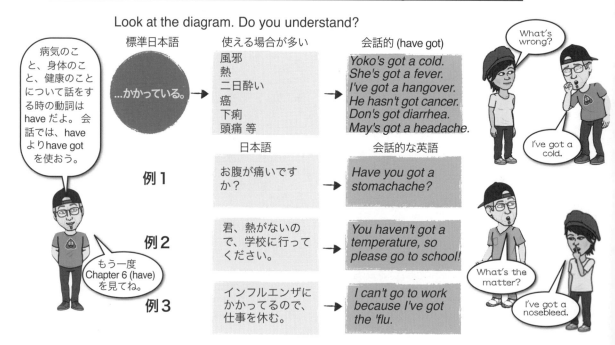

What's the matter?
I've got a nosebleed.

LEARN THESE SENTENCES

5　...薬を飲んで...　Take ... tablets ...

Look at the diagram. Do you understand?

薬を飲む、という動詞はtake だよ。病院や薬局で薬を出してくれるとき、いつ、どれだけの量を飲むのかを教えてくれるよね。

Please take 2 tablets after each meal.
And 2 tablets before each meal.
...

日本語	基本	キーワード
薬を飲む →	Take ... tablets ... (pills) (capsules) →	before / after / between / each — meal(s)

	日本語	会話的な英語
例 1	４時間ごとに、カプセルを１錠飲みなさい。 →	*Take 1 capsule every 4 hours.*
例 2	夕食の前、カプセルを１錠飲みなさい。 →	*Take 1 capsule before dinner.*
例 3	一日２回食間、錠剤を２錠飲みなさい。 →	*Take 2 tablets between meals, twice a day.*
例 4	一日３回 食事後、錠剤を３錠飲みなさい。 →	*Take 3 pills after meals, 3 times a day.*
例 5	毎日毎食後、錠剤を３錠飲みなさい。 →	*Take 3 pills after each meal daily.*

Take 3 pills before meals 3 times a day.
You mean take 3 pills before each meal daily?

6　回復した。　I'm better.

Look at the diagram. Do you understand?

標準日本語	標準英語	会話的
回復した。 →	I recovered. →	*I'm better.* / *I feel better.*

例	A: 風邪はどう？ B: もう治った！ →	A: *How's your cold?* B: *I'm better now!*

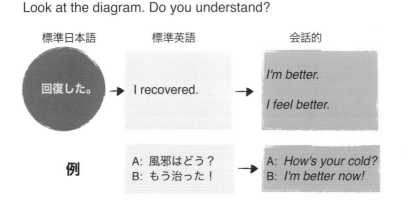

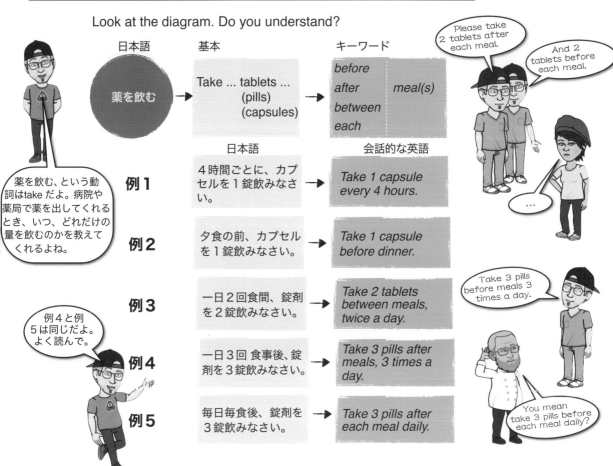

I'm better now!

CHALLENGE STAGE

Challenge 1. *Fill in the blanks from the list.*

1 Sherlock: Hello. Doctor Watson?

2 Doctor: Yes. あなたは...

3 Sherlock: Groans. Sherlock Groans. 11時30分に予約をしています。

4 Doctor: Well. It's 11:30 now, so come into my office.

5 *(Sherlock and Dr Watson go into Dr Watson's office.)*

6 Doctor: グローンズさん、どうしましたか？

7 Sherlock: Well, I've got a very bad cough.

8 Doctor: I see. Have you got a headache?

9 Sherlock: Yes. And I've also got a sore throat.

10 Doctor: Hmm. 熱と血圧を測りましょう。

11 Sherlock: Okay.

12 Doctor: Hmm. 37.5 degrees. 熱がありますよ。 You've also got high blood pressure.

13 Sherlock: What's wrong with me, Doctor? 重いのですか？

14 Doctor: No, Mr Groans. It's not serious. I'll give you some medicine.

15 Sherlock: ワトソン先生、ありがとうございます。何が問題なのですか？
What's wrong with me?

16 Doctor: Mr Groans. You smoke too much. Stop smoking your pipe.
Here's your medicine. 家へ帰って、休みなさい。

Choose the best sentence for the blanks:

a) You've got a temperature.
b) Go home and rest.
c) Is it serious?
d) And you are . . . ?
e) Thanks Dr Watson, but what's the problem?
f) What seems to be the problem, Mr Groans?
g) I'll take your temperature and blood pressure.
h) I have an appointment to see you at 11:30.

CHALLENGE STAGE

Challenge 2. *Circle the correct answer.*

1. You go to Dr Spock's office for the first time. You say *Hello. Dr Spock?* He says;
   (a) Yes. I've met you before. (b) Yes. I know your name.
   (c) Yes. And you are . . . ? (d) Yes. Live long and prosper.

2. If you want to go to the clinic, or see the dentist, you often NEED;
   (a) a point (b) an appointment
   (c) a disappoint (d) a disappointment

3. When you go into the doctor's office, the doctor will say:
   (a) Is there a problem? (b) Do you have a problem?
   (c) What seems to be the problem? (d) What's your problem?

4. Which of the following does NOT mean *What's the matter?*
   (a) What's the bad? (b) What's the trouble?
   (c) What's the problem? (d) What's wrong?

5. If your head hurts, you should say:
   (a) I am a headache. (b) I've got a headache.
   (c) I gotta' have a headache. (d) I have a head.

6. Which sentence is NOT the same as *I caught a cold*?
   (a) I have a cold. (b) I have got a cold.
   (c) I am cold. (d) I've got a cold.

7. Which question is the same as *Do you have a stomachache?* (腹痛)
   (a) You are a stomachache? (b) Are you a stomachache?
   (c) Do you stomachache? (d) Have you got a stomachache?

8. If the doctor says *You haven't got a temperature*, the meaning is;
   (a) Your temperature is normal. (b) Your temperature is too low.
   (c) Your temperature is high. (d) You are dead.

9. Take 2 tablets before meals, 3 times a day is the same as:
   (a) Take 2 tablets after meals, 3 times a day. (b) Take 3 tablets before meals, 2 times a day.
   (c) Take 2 tablets before meals, 3 days a week. (d) Take 2 tablets before each meal daily.

10. When your cold has gone(回復した), you can say:
   (a) I'm better now. (b) I'm in recovery mode.
   (c) I am not cold now. (d) I recovered my body.

CHALLENGE STAGE

Challenge 3. *Did you read the English story?*
Let's check!

1. What time is Yoko's appointment?
   - *(i)* *Yoko's appointment is 3 o'clock.*
   - *(ii)* *Yoko's appointment is 3:30.*
   - *(iii)* *Yoko's appointment is 4 o'clock.*
   - *(iv)* *Yoko's appointment is 4:30.*

2. When Yoko woke up, how did she feel?
   - *(i)* *When she woke up, she felt good.*
   - *(ii)* *When she woke up, she felt excited.*
   - *(iii)* *When she woke up, she felt sick.*
   - *(iv)* *When she woke up, she felt tired.*

3. When Yoko woke up, she had;
   - *(i)* *a stomachache.*
   - *(ii)* *a toothache.*
   - *(iii)* *a nice dream.*
   - *(iv)* *no money.*

4. How is Yoko's headache?
   - *(i)* *She has a very bad headache.*
   - *(ii)* *She has a bad headache.*
   - *(iii)* *She has a slight headache.*
   - *(iv)* *She doesn't have a headache.*

5. What is Yoko's temperature?
   - *(i)* *Her temperature is 39.9 degrees.*
   - *(ii)* *Her temperature is 37.9 degrees.*
   - *(iii)* *Her temperature is 37.3 degrees.*
   - *(iv)* *Her temperature is 33.7 degrees.*

6. When did Yoko have diarrhea?
   - *(i)* *She had diarrhea last night.*
   - *(ii)* *She had diarrhea this morning.*
   - *(iii)* *She had diarrhea everyday.*
   - *(iv)* *She didn't have diarrhea.*

7. How many drinks did Yoko say she had?
   - *(i)* *She said she had 6 or 7 drinks.*
   - *(ii)* *She said she had 4 or 5 drinks.*
   - *(iii)* *She said she had 3 or 4 drinks.*
   - *(iv)* *She said she didn't drink.*

8. How is Yoko's blood pressure?
   - *(i)* *She's got high blood pressure.*
   - *(ii)* *She's got low blood pressure.*
   - *(iii)* *She's got usual blood pressure.*
   - *(iv)* *She has no blood pressure.*

9. What is wrong with Yoko? Why is she sick?
   - *(i)* *She's got the 'flu (influenza).*
   - *(ii)* *She's got a very bad cold.*
   - *(iii)* *She's got a hangover.*
   - *(iv)* *She ate too much.*

10. How many times did Yoko throw up?
    - *(i)* *She threw up once.*
    - *(ii)* *She threw up twice.*
    - *(iii)* *She threw up three times.*
    - *(iv)* *She didn't throw up. Ladies never throw up.*

"Never heard of it."

QUICK START

したことがある	...したことがありますか？ ...したことある？ いや。ありません。 うん。あります。	*Have you ever ... ?* *You ever ... ?* *No, I've never ...* *Yes, I've ...*	**Have you ever...**
結構	結構暑いです。 彼女はかなり若いです。 彼はなんか、頭が良いです。 少し疲れて見えます。	*It's pretty hot.* *She's fairly young.* *He's kinda smart.* *You look a bit tired.*	***pretty/fairly***
のよう...	彼について知っていることを教えてください。(どういう人?) 彼は何が好きですか。 彼はどのように見えますか？	*What is he like?* *What does he like?* *What does he look like?*	***It's like ...***
ほら...	ええと... (知っているけれど思い出せない)	*You know ...*	***You know...***

You got it? (分かった？)

☺

- もう分かりましたか？
- チャレンジをやってみよう。
- *10f, 10g & 10h (ページ98~100)*にトライしよう。

- ***You got it?***
- ***Try the challenge section:***
- ***Exercises 10f, 10g, 10h (pages 98~100)***

☹

- まだ分かりませんか？
- まず、*10b, 10c, 10d & 10e*を読んで*(ページ92~97)*
- *10f, 10g & 10h (ページ98~100)*にトライしよう。

- ***You don't get it? Not sure?***
- ***Read Sections 10b, 10c, 10d & 10e (pages 92~97)***
- ***Then, try exercises 10f, 10g, 10h (pages 98~100)***

10b
経験

THE ENGLISH STORY

Experiences - Yoko and John discuss their experiences.

1 Yoko: *Hi John. I feel terrible.*

2 John: *The doctor said you've got a pretty bad[1] hangover.*

3 Yoko: *Yeah. Have you ever had a bad hangover before?[2]*

4 John: *No, I've never had one before.*

5 Yoko *Really?*

6 John: *Ha ha. Just joking! Of course I've had one before.*

7 Yoko: *When?*

8 John: *Well ... Have you ever been to Al's Bar?*

9 Yoko *No, I've never been there.*

10 John: *Well ... last week I went there and I drank 23 bottles of stout.*

11 Yoko: *Stout? What is stout like?[3]*

12 John: *Stout ... you know ...[4] Stout is like black beer. Haven't you ever drunk stout?*

13 Yoko: *No, I've never drunk it.*

14 John: *Well ... I drank 23 bottles of stout and I had a bad hangover the next day.*

15 Yoko: *Twenty three bottles?*

16 John: *Yeah, but have you ever met my two friends, George and Paul?*

17 Yoko: *Yes, I've met them.*

18 John: *Well ... last Tuesday night, they each drank 48 mugs of beer at Al's Bar. On Wednesday morning, they had terrible hangovers.*

19 Yoko: *In Japan, I often drank nigori saki. Have you ever tried nigori saki?*

20 John: *No. I've never heard of it and I've never tried it.*

21 Yoko: *It's very strong.*

22 John: *Yoko?*

23 Yoko: *Yes John?*

24 John: *We both drink too much.*

Simon Says - Easy Conversational English

THE JAPANESE STORY

10c
経験

経験 - ヨーコとジョンは色々な経験について話します。

1 ヨーコ: ハーイ、ジョン。私、サイテーよ。

2 ジョン: 先生が君は結構ひどい[1]二日酔いだったって言ってたよ。

3 ヨーコ: そうなの。二日酔いになったことある？[2]

4 ジョン: ないよ。一度もない。

5 ヨーコ: ほんと？

6 ジョン: ハハハ、冗談さ。もちろんなったことがあるよ。

7 ヨーコ: いつ？

8 ジョン: えーと ... アルズ・バーに行ったことあるかい？

9 ヨーコ: いいえ、一度もないわ。

10 ジョン: あのさ ... 先週そこに行ってスタウトを２３本飲んだんだよ。

11 ヨーコ: スタウト？ スタウトってどういうもの？[3]

12 ジョン: スタウトはね ... ほら ...[4]スタウトは黒ビールみたいなものさ。スタウトを飲んだことはないの？

13 ヨーコ: ええ、一度も飲んだことがないわ。

14 ジョン: とにかく、僕はさ、スタウトを２３本飲んで、次の日ひどい二日酔いになったよ。

15 ヨーコ: ２３本か...

16 ジョン: そうだね。でも僕の友達のジョージとポールに会ったことあるかい？

17 ヨーコ: ええ、会ったことあるわ。

18 ジョン: あのね ... 火曜の夜、アルズ・バーであいつらジョッキで４８杯ずつビールを飲んだんだよ。水曜の朝、二人ともひどい二日酔いだったよ。

19 ヨーコ: 日本では、私はよく「にごり酒」を飲むのよ。「にごり酒」を試したことある？

20 ジョン: いいや、聞いたことないし試したこともないよ。

21 ヨーコ: とてもきつい（アルコール分が強い）のよ。

22 ジョン: ヨーコさあ ...

23 ヨーコ: なあに、ジョン？

24 ヨーコ: 僕らは二人とも飲みすぎだね。

10d
経験

Simon Says - Easy Conversational English

EXAMPLES

A: Have you ever eaten caviar?
B: No, I've never eaten it.

* * *

A: Have you ever been to France before?
B: No, I've never been there.

* * *

A: Have you ever driven a car?
B: Yes, of course I've driven one.

* * *

A: You ever heard of Marilyn Monroe?
B: Nah, never heard of her.

* * *

A: It's fairly late. Let's go home!
B: Yeah, I'm pretty sleepy.
A: I'm kinda tired too.

* * *

A: What is she like?
B: She's pretty tall and fairly pretty.

* * *

A: What does she like?
B: She likes cake.

My dog's pretty pretty.

* * *

A: What is sashimi like?
B: Sashimi?
A: Yeah ... you know ... raw fish.
B: Oh, it's a tasty Japanese food.

* * *

A: How many years ago Did John die?
B: John? John Who?.
A: John ... you know ... John Lennon!

A: キャビアを食べたことがありますか？
B: いいえ、一回も食べたことはありません。

* * *

A: フランスへ行ったことがありますか？
B: いいえ、一度も行ったことがありません。

* * *

A: 車を運転したことがありますか？
B: ええ、もちろん運転したことがあります。

* * *

A: マリリン・モンロー、聞いたことある？
B: いや、彼女のことは 知らないな。

* * *

A: かなり遅くなったね。帰ろう！
B: うん。結構眠いです。
A: 僕もなんか、ちょっと疲れてるよ。

* * *

A: 彼女はどういう人ですか？
B: 結構背が高くて、かなりきれいです。

* * *

A: 彼女は何が好きですか？
B: 彼女はケーキが好きですね。

あの犬は結構可愛い…

* * *

A: サシミってどういうものですか？
B: サシミですか？
A: ええ、ほらほら、あれ、 生の魚！
B: あぁ、おいしい日本の料理だよ。

* * *

A: ジョンは何年前に亡くなったの？
B: ジョン？ ジョンって誰？
A: ほら…あの人さ、ジョン・レノン。

LEARN THESE SENTENCES

1 ... 結構ひどい... ... pretty bad....

Look at the diagram. Do you understand?

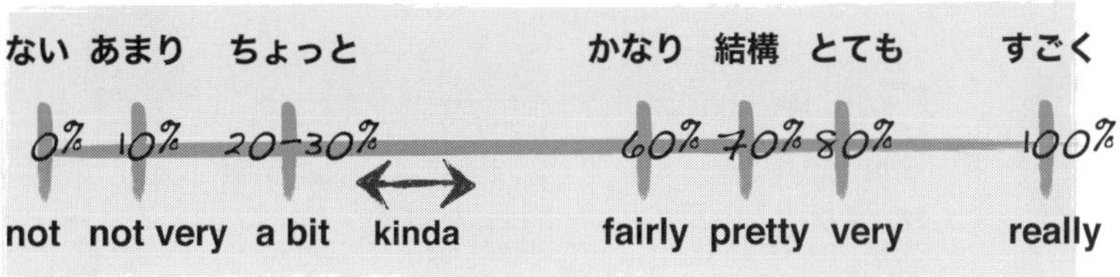

ない あまり ちょっと かなり 結構 とても すごく
0% 10% 20-30% 60% 70% 80% 100%
not not very a bit kinda fairly pretty very really

This is pretty important. Please read it.

日本語		英語
結構寒いです。	→	*It's pretty cold.*
彼はかなりお金持ちです。	→	*He's fairly rich.*
僕の靴はちょっと小さいです。	→	*My shoes are a bit small.*
日本語はなんか難しいですね。	→	*Japanese is kinda' difficult.*

a bit と a little bit は同じだよ。kindaも同じような表現だ。
もう一度 ４５ページを 見てね。

I'm kinda drunk too!
I'm fairly drunk!

2 ...したことがある？ Have you ever ...？

Look at the diagram. Do you understand?

標準日本語	標準英語		会話的
...したことがありますか？	Have you ever ... ? Have you ever ... before? Have you ... before? Have you ...?	→	*Have you ever ...?* *You ever ...?*

	日本語		英語
例１	ドリアンを食べたことがありますか？	→	*Have you ever eaten durian?*
例２	沖縄に行ったことがある？	→	*You ever been to Okinawa?*

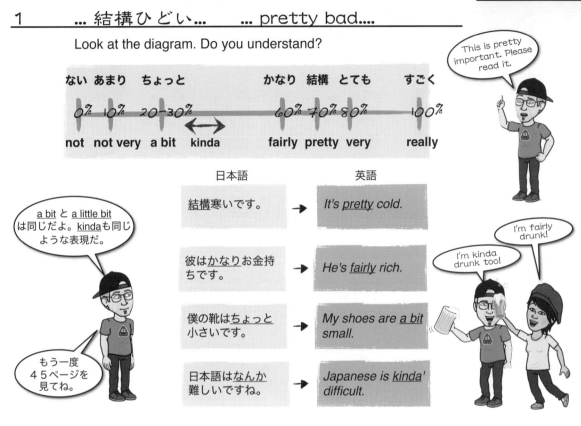

質問は、You everで始まると、会話的になるよ。

You ever seen a ghost?
No, I haven't.

10e
経験

LEARN THESE SENTENCES

Look at the diagram. Do you understand?

日本語	質問		答え
省略 →	Have you ever played **golf**?	→	*Yes. I've played **it**.*
	Have you ever seen **a** UFO?	→	*No, I've never seen **one**.*
	Have you ever been to **Tokyo**?	→	*Yes, I've been **there**.*

	言葉		省略
要するに	場所	→	*there*
	男		*him*
	女		*her*
	２人以上		*them*
	aに付く言葉」		*one*
	他の言葉		*it*
例１	じゅん子に会ったことがありますか？	→	*Have you ever met **Junko**?*
	いや。会ったことはありません。		*Nope. I've never met **her**.*
例２	UFOを見たことがありますか？	→	*Have you ever seen **a** UFO?*
	いや。見たことはありません。		*No. I've never seen **one**.*

	質問		長い答え
答え方 →	Have you ever eaten **fugu**?	→	*Yes. I've eaten **it**.*
	Have you ever eaten **fugu**?		*No, I've never eaten **it**.*

質問		短い答え
Have you ever eaten **fugu**?	→	*Yes, I have.*
Have you ever eaten **fugu**?		*No, I haven't.*

	日本語		会話的な英語
例１ (長い)	アマゾンに行ったことがある？	→	*You ever been to the **Amazon**?*
	いいえ。行ったことがない。		*Nah. I've never been **there**.*
例２ (短い)	AKB48を見たことがありますか？	→	*Have you ever seen AKB 48?*
	はい、あります。		*Yes, I have.*

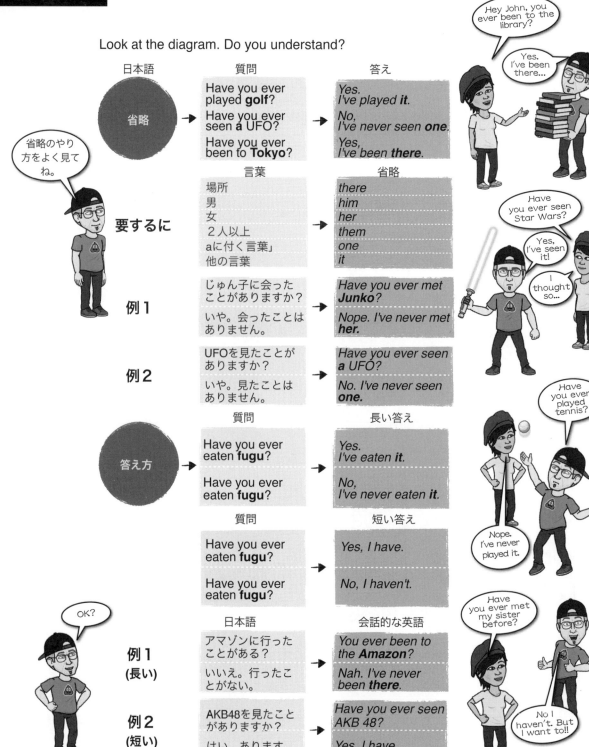

経験

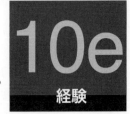

LEARN THESE SENTENCES

3   …ってどのような…ですか？   What is …. like?

Look at the diagram. Do you understand?

ポイント	日本語	会話的な英語
どのような… →	彼女、どういう人ですか？ 彼女はどのような人ですか？	*What is she like?*

What does he like?

He likes beer!

質問は似てるかもしれないけど、意味は全く違うので、気をつけよう。

比べて

間違わないように…

彼、どういう人です？	*What **is** he **like**?*
彼は何が好きですか？	*What **does** he **like**?*
彼はどのように見えますか？	*What **does** he **look** **like**?*

What is he like?

Well...he's old, bald and likes playing games.

	日本語	英語
is like	ジョンって、どういう人ですか？	*What is John like?*
	若くて背が高くて、おもしろい人です。	*He's a young, tall funny guy.*
like	ジョンは何が好きなの？	*What does John like?*
	ジョンはビールが好きですよ。	*He likes beer!*
look like	ジョンはどのように見えますか？	*What does John look like?*
	ブルース・ウィリスみたい！	*He looks likes Bruce Willis.*

You look like a chef.

I AM a chef!

4   … ええと……   … you know …

Look at the diagram. Do you understand?

「ええと…」という意味だよ。っているけれど思い出せないときに使うよ。

ポイント	日本語	英語
相槌	…ほら… ええと… …あれ、わかるよね …なんだっけ？… …それ…	… *you know* … … *y'know* …
例	A: あれ、ドアを空けるやつ…何だっけ…ほら… わかるでしょう？ B: 鍵のことですか？ A: そう。鍵だ！	A: *What's that thing … you know... for opening doors.* B: *You mean a key?* A: *Yeah, a key!*

What do you want to eat tonight?

Anything is fine.

How 'bout round bread?

What?

You know... round bread!

Oh!! You mean pizza?! OK.

CHALLENGE STAGE

Challenge 1. *Fill in the blanks from the list.*

1 Eve: Haven't you ever eaten an apple?

2 Adam: いいえ、1回も食べたことはありません。

3 Eve: Apples are wonderful. They are good for you. I eat them all the time.

4 Adam: Really? What about juice? Have you ever drunk apple juice?

5 Eve: はい、飲んだことがありますよ。 How about you?

6 Adam: いいえ、1回も飲んだことはありません。

7 Eve: Have you ever eaten apple pie?

8 Adam: いいえ、1回も食べたことはありません。 What about you?

9 Eve: はい、食べたことがあります。 Have you ever eaten at the Big Apple Restaurant?

10 Adam: いいえ、1回もそこで食べたことはありません。

11 Eve: I see. Have you ever been to Eden Park?

12 Adam: いいえ、1回も行ったことがありません。 Eve, have you ever seen a snake?

13 ! Eve: いいえ、見たことがないんです。 Why?

14 Adam: There's a big one in that apple tree!

Choose the best sentence for the blanks:

a) No, I've never been there.

b) No, I haven't ever eaten one.

c) No, I've never seen one.

d) Yes, I've drunk it.

e) No, I've never ever eaten it.

f) No, I haven't ever eaten there.

g) No, I've never drunk it.

h) Yes, I've eaten it.

CHALLENGE STAGE

Challenge 2. *Circle the correct answer.*

1. Which of the following is NOT a good answer to *Are you tired?*
   (a) I'm pretty tired. (b) I'm fairly tired.
   (c) I'm really tired. (d) I'm radial tired.

2. The expression (表現) *It's kinda late,* is similar to:
   (a) It's very late. (b) It's not late.
   (c) It's a bit late. (d) It's really late.

3. Which question means the same as *Have you ever been to England?*
   (a) Have ever been to England? (b) Have you ever go to England?
   (c) Have you going to England? (d) Have you been to England before?

4. Which question means the same as *Have you ever eaten blue cheese?*
   (a) Eaten to blue cheese? (b) You ever eaten blue cheese?
   (c) You ever blue cheese? (d) Have to ever eat blue cheese?

5. The question is - *Have you ever eaten raw fish?* The best answer is:
   (a) Yes, I've eaten one. (b) Yes, I've eaten there.
   (c) Yes, I've eaten it. (d) Yes, I've eaten them.

6. The question is - *Haven't you ever seen a horror movie?* The best answer is:
   (a) Yes, I've seen one. (b) Yes, I've seen there.
   (c) Yes, I've seen it. (d) Yes, I've seen them.

7. The question is - *Have you ever listened to The Beatles?* The best answer is:
   (a) Yes, I've listened to them. (b) Yes, I've listened to it.
   (c) Yes, I've listened to him. (d) Yes, I've listened to there.

8. The answer is - *She's young, clever, fairly tall and likes cooking.* What is the question?
   (a) What does Jane look like? (b) What is Jane like?
   (c) What does Jane like? (d) What are Jane's like?

9. The question is - *What does Doraemon look like?* The best answer is:
   (a) He looks a cat with no ears. (b) He looks like a cat with no ears.
   (c) He likes a cat with no ears. (d) He does a cat with no ears.

10. John and Yoko are having dinner together at a Japanese restaurant.
    John says *What is okonomiyaki?* Yoko explains. She says:
    (a) *Okonomiyaki* ... I know ... cabbage pancake. (b) *Okonomiyaki* ... Osaka ... cabbage pancake.
    (c) *Okonomiyaki* ... you know ... cabbage pancake. (d) *Okonomiyaki* ... don't know ... cabbage pancake.

CHALLENGE STAGE

Challenge 3. *Did you read the English story?*
Let's check!

1.	How does Yoko feel?	*(i)*	*She feels great.*
		(ii)	*She feels cool.*
		(iii)	*She feels happy.*
		(iv)	*She feels terrible.*
2.	Where did John go last week?	*(i)*	*He went to Al's Bar.*
		(ii)	*He went to Yoko's house.*
		(iii)	*He went to the supermarket.*
		(iv)	*He went to hospital.*
3.	How many bottles of stout did John drink last week?	*(i)*	*He drank 32 bottles.*
		(ii)	*He drank 22 bottles.*
		(iii)	*He drank 23 bottles.*
		(iv)	*He drank 12 bottles.*
4.	What is stout like?	*(i)*	*Stout is like sweet beer.*
		(ii)	*Stout is like black beer.*
		(iii)	*Stout is like fat beer.*
		(iv)	*Stout is like draft beer.*
5.	What are the names of John's two friends?	*(i)*	*Their names are George and Ringo.*
		(ii)	*Their names are Ringo and Paul.*
		(iii)	*Their names are George and Paul.*
		(iv)	*Their names are Paul and Al.*
6.	When did John's two friends go drinking?	*(i)*	*They went drinking on Tuesday night.*
		(ii)	*They went drinking on Thursday night.*
		(iii)	*They went drinking on Friday night.*
		(iv)	*They went drinking on Saturday night.*
7.	How many mugs of beer did John's two friends each drink?	*(i)*	*They each drank 48 mugs.*
		(ii)	*They each drank 84 mugs.*
		(iii)	*They each drank 14 mugs.*
		(iv)	*They each drank 18 mugs.*
8.	On Wednesday, John's two friends had;	*(i)*	*nice memories.*
		(ii)	*terrible hangovers.*
		(iii)	*matching pajamas.*
		(iv)	*no money.*
9.	In Japan, what did Yoko often drink?	*(i)*	*In Japan, she often drank green tea.*
		(ii)	*In Japan, she often drank can coffee.*
		(iii)	*In Japan, she often drank cheap wine.*
		(iv)	*In Japan, she often drank nigori saki.*
10.	Finally, what does John say to Yoko?	*(i)*	*He says, we both talk too much.*
		(ii)	*He says, we both play too much.*
		(iii)	*He says, we both drink too much.*
		(iv)	*He says, we both eat too much.*

"In 2 weeks?"

２週間後、
私は帰ります。
再来週ですか？

I'm leaving in two weeks.
The week after next?

QUICK START

ごめん	お待たせしてすみません。 遅れてごめんなさい。 遅れてごめんね。	*Sorry I kept you waiting.* *I'm sorry I'm late.* *Sorry I'm late.*	***Sorry ...***
前・後	５分前 約５分前 ５分後・後５分 約５分後 ５分後・後５分	*5 minutes ago* *about 5 minutes ago* *in 5 minutes* *in about 5 minutes* *in 5 minutes' time*	***ago/in***
再来・先々	明後日（あさって） 一昨日（おととい） 再来週 先々月	*the day after tomorrow* *the day before yesterday* *the week after next* *the month before last*	***before/after***
何回目	２回目 ２回	*the/my second time* *two times/twice*	***1st/2nd time***

You got it? (分かった？)

☺

- もう分かりましたか？
- チャレンジをやってみよう。
- *11f, 11g & 11h (ページ108~110)*にトライしよう。

- ***You got it?***
- ***Try the challenge section:***
- ***Exercises 11f, 11g, 11h (pages 108~110)***

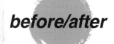

Yes
OR
No

☹

- まだ分かりませんか？
- まず、*11b, 11c, 11d & 11e*を読んで*(ページ102~107)*
- *11f, 11g & 11h (ページ108~110)*にトライしよう。

- ***You don't get it? Not sure?***
- ***Read Sections 11b, 11c, 11d & 11e (pages 102~107)***
- ***Then, try exercises 11f, 11g, 11h (pages108~110)***

THE ENGLISH STORY

Past and future - John talks to Yoko in a café.

1 John: *Hi Yoko. I'm sorry I kept you waiting.*[1]

2 Yoko: *That's okay. I only arrived 5 minutes ago.*[2]

3 John: *Yeah? I left home an hour ago, but there was a big traffic jam.*

4 Yoko: *No problem.*

5 John: *This is a nice café. Do you come here often?*

6 Yoko: *No. Today is only my second time.*[3] *I first came here 4 days ago with Paul and Linda.*

7 John: *Really? I'm meeting Paul in about 2 hours.*[4] *It's Ringo's birthday in 2 days' time, so we're buying him a present.*

8 Yoko: *In 2 days' time? The day after tomorrow?*[5]

9 John: *Yep, that's right. The day after tomorrow. We wanted to have a party, but Ringo's in London.*

10 Yoko: *In London? When did he go there?*

11 John: *He went there 6 days ago.*

12 Yoko: *When does he come back?*

13 John: *He comes back in about 10 days.*

14 Yoko: *I see. By the way John, when is your birthday?*

15 John: *My birthday? My birthday was about 5 months ago. What about you, Yoko? When is your birthday?*

16 Yoko: *My birthday is in about 2 weeks' time.*

17 John: *The week after next?*[6] *Great, let's have a big birthday party.*

18 Yoko: *Good idea John, but there's a small problem.*

19 John: *A small problem? What?*

20 Yoko: *Umm ... I'm going back to Japan in 2 weeks.*

THE JAPANESE STORY

11c
過去未来

過去未来 - ジョンはカフェでヨーコと話します。

1　ジョン：　やあ、ヨーコ。ごめん、待たせちゃったね。¹

2　ヨーコ：　全然。5分前に着いたばかりだから。²

3　ジョン：　そうかい？　1時間前に家を出たんだけど、ひどい交通渋滞があったんだ。

4　ヨーコ：　構わないわ。

5　ジョン：　いい店（喫茶店）だね。よく来るの？

6　ヨーコ：　そうでもないわ、今日で2回目よ。³ 4日前にポールとリンダといっしょに初めて来たの。

7　ジョン：　へえ？　2時間くらい⁴ したらポールと会うんだ。リンゴの誕生日が2日後なんだ。それでプレゼントを買いに行くんだよ。

8　ヨーコ：　2日後？　あさってってこと？⁵

9　ジョン：　そう、その通り。あさってだよ。僕らはパーティーをやりたかったんだけど、リンゴはロンドンにいるんだ。

10　ヨーコ：　ロンドンに？　いつ行ったの？

11　ジョン：　6日前だよ。

12　ヨーコ：　いつ帰ってくるのかしら？

13　ジョン：　10日後に帰ってくるよ。

14　ヨーコ：　わかったわ。ジョン、ところであなたの誕生日はいつなの？

15　ジョン：　僕の誕生日かい？　僕の誕生日は5ヶ月前だよ。ヨーコは？　君の誕生日はいつ？

16　ヨーコ：　2週間くらい後よ。

17　ジョン：　再来週かい？⁶ よーし、ばーんと誕生日パーティーをしようよ。

18　ヨーコ：　グッド・アイディアね、ジョン。でもちょっと問題があるわ。

19　ジョン：　問題？　何だい？

20　ヨーコ：　あの... 2週間後に日本に帰るの。

11d
過去未来

A: I'm sorry I kept you waiting.
B: That's okay.

* * *

A: I'm sorry I'm late.
B: No problem.

* * *

A: When did the movie finish?
B: About 30 seconds ago.

* * *

A: When did you buy your car?
B: I bought it about 8 or 9 years ago.

* * *

A: What time are you leaving?
B: I'm leaving in 5 minutes.

* * *

A: When do you graduate?
B: I graduate in 3 months' time.

* * *

A: When are you moving?
B: The day after tomorrow.

* * *

A: When are you going to Tokyo?
B: I'm going the month after next.

* * *

A: When did they get married?
B: The year before last.

* * *

A: How many times have you been married?
B: This is my ninth time.

A: お待たせしてごめんなさいね。
B: 構いませんよ。

* * *

A: 遅くなってごめんね。
B: 構いませんよ。

* * *

A: 映画は、いつ終わったの？
B: ３０秒くらい前だよ。

* * *

A: いつ車を買ったの？
B: ８年か９年くらい前に買った。

* * *

A: 何時に出るの？
B: ５分後に出ます。

* * *

A: いつ卒業するの？
B: ３ヶ月後に卒業します。

* * *

A: いつ引越しするの？
B: あさってです。

* * *

A: いつ東京へ行くの？
B: 再来月に行きます。

* * *

A: あいつらは、いつ結婚したの？
B: おとといです。

* * *

A: 今までに何回結婚したことがありますか？
B: 今は９回目です。

LEARN THESE SENTENCES

1　　お待たせしました。 I'm sorry I kept you waiting.

Look at the diagram. Do you understand?

標準日本語	標準英語	会話的
お待たせ しました。	I'm sorry I kept you waiting. I'm sorry to have kept you waiting. I'm sorry to keep you waiting.	I'm sorry I'm late. Sorry I'm late.

	日本語	英語
丁寧	お待たせして申し訳ありません。	I'm sorry to have kept you waiting.
普通	遅れてごめんなさい。	I'm sorry I'm late.
フレンドリー	遅れてごめんね。	Sorry I'm late.

Sorry I'm late.

...

2　　５分前... 　　5 minutes ago...

Look at the diagram. Do you understand?

ポイント	日本語	英語
前	1秒前 2分前 3時間前 4日前 5週間前 6ヶ月前　　など	1 second ago 2 minutes ago 3 hours ago 4 days ago 5 weeks ago 6 months ago　etc

	日本語	英語
例1	約３０年前、私は日本に来ました。	I came to Japan about **30 years ago.**
例2	僕の誕生日は５ヶ月前でした。	My birthday was **5 months ago.**
例3	２年くらい前に、車を買いました。	I bought my car about **2 years ago.**
例4	１時間前、家を出ました。	I left home **an hour ago.**

単語の順番は日本語と同じだよ。
2時間前は 2 days ago だよ。

When did you start running?

About 2 hours ago.

When did you catch a cold?

About 3 days ago.

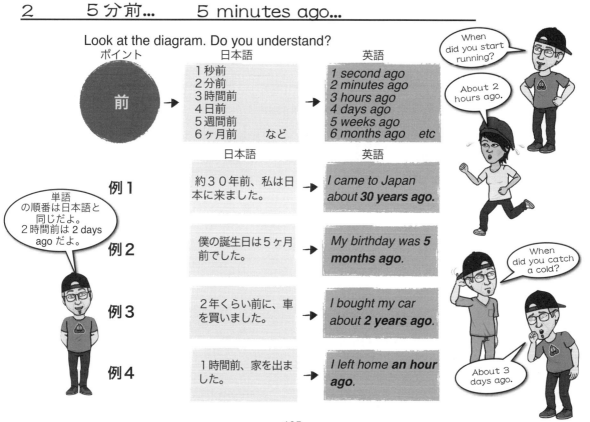

LEARN THESE SENTENCES

3   …2回目です   … my second time

Look at the diagram. Do you understand?

日本語	何回	何回目
何回 vs 何回目	I have been here **4 times**. The boxer was KOed **10 times**! She has eaten fugu at least **10 times**.	This is **the 4th time**. It was **his 10th time**. It is at least **her 10th time**.

How many times have you called her today?

This is the 10th time!

	日本語	英語
例1	京都には何回行ったことがありますか？ 6回行ったことがあります。	How many times have you been to Kyoto? I've been there **6 times**.
例2	何回授業をサボったの？ 今回は8回目です。	How many times did you cut class? This is the **8th time**.
例3	フグは食べたことがない。 私は3回食べたことがあるけど、初めて食べたのは去年だったよ。	I've never eaten fugu. I've eaten it 3 times, but last year was the 1st time.

何回目の話をするとき、 the でも my でも、どちらでもいいよ。例えば、my first time と the first time は同じだよ。

John didn't come!

This is the 3rd time!

4   …2時間後   … in 2 hours (in 2 hours' time)

Look at the diagram. Do you understand?

ポイント	日本語	英語
後	1秒後 2分後 3時間後 4日後 5週間後 6ヶ月後 など	in 1 second in 2 minutes in 3 hours in 4 days in 5 weeks in 6 months etc

Please hurry! We're leaving in 2 hours' time.

time を使うときは、アポストロフィ (')の位置に気つけてね。単数形は 1 week's time、複数形は2 weeks' time.

	日本語	英語
例1	僕の誕生日は5ヶ月後です。	My birthday is in 5 months' time.
例2	約2時間後、ポールと会います。	I'm meeting Paul in about 2 hours.
例3	1、2時間後、雨は止むでしょう。	The rain will stop in an hour or two.

Really? In 2 hours? I don't know what to wear...

When is your dancing contest?

It's in 2 days! I have to practice!

LEARN THESE SENTENCES

5   明後日   the day after tomorrow

Look at the diagram. Do you understand?

一昨日
(おととい)

明後日
(あさって)

単語の順番

the day	**before**	yesterday
(日)	(前)	(昨日)
つまり 昨日	の 前 の	日
the day	**after**	tomorrow
(日)	(後)	(明日)
つまり 明日	の 後 の	日

OK?

	日本語		英語
例1	おととい、私は新しいスター・ウォーズの映画を見たんだ。	→	*I watched the new Star Wars movie the day before yesterday.*
例2	私達はあさって出発します。	→	*We're leaving the day after tomorrow.*
例3	僕の誕生日はあさってです。彼女のはおとといでした。	→	*My birthday is the day after tomorrow. Hers was the day before yesterday.*

You look sad...

Yeah. I'm going to the dentist the day after tomorrow.

You didn't come to my party!

I forgot. When was it?

It was the day before yesterday.

6   再来週   the week after next

Look at the diagram. Do you remember the pattern?

単語の順番

先々...

再来...

	week (週)		
the	*month* (月)	**before**	**last**
	year (年)		
	week (週)		
the	*month* (月)	**after**	**next**
	year (年)		

パターンと単語の並びは「明後日」と「一昨日」と同じです。

	日本語	英語
例1	私は一昨年新しい車を買いました。	*I bought a new car the year before last.*
例2	彼女は再来週出発します。	*She's leaving the week after next.*
例3	僕の誕生日は再来月です。	*My birthday is the month after next.*

When are you going back to Japan?

I'm leaving the month after next.

When was your first strange mail?

Maybe the week before last.

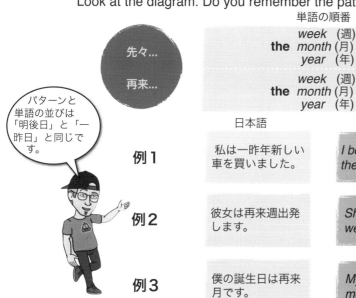

CHALLENGE STAGE

Challenge 1. *Fill in the blanks from the list.*

1 Fred: Hi Barney. 遅れて、ごめんね。

2 Barney: いいですよ。 I only arrived 10 minutes ago.

3 Fred: Really. I left home an hour ago, but the road was very crowded.

4 Barney: No problem.

5 Fred: I have to meet Wilma in an hour. It's Dino's birthday in 2 days' time so we're buying him a present.

6 Barney: ２日後？ The day after tomorrow?

7 Fred: That's right. あさってですよ。

8 Barney: What about you Fred? 君の誕生日はいつですか？

9 Fred: My birthday? 僕の誕生日は２ヶ月後ですよ。

10 Barney: Really? In 2 months?

11 Fred: Yeah, that's right. バーニーさんの誕生日はいつですか？

12 Barney: 僕の誕生日は一週間前だよ。

13 Fred: Oh. Last week? I'm sorry I didn't get you a present.

14 Barney: That's okay, Fred.

Choose the best sentence for the blanks:

a) So, when is your birthday, Barney?
b) In 2 days?
c) That's okay.
d) My birthday was one week ago.
e) Sorry I'm late.
f) The day after tomorrow?
g) My birthday is in 2 months' time.
h) When is your birthday?

CHALLENGE STAGE

Challenge 2. *Circle the correct answer.*

1. If you are late to a meeting, you should say:
   (a) I'm sorry you kept me waiting. (b) I'm sorry I kept you waiting.
   (c) I'm sorry you're late. (d) I'm very sorry lately.

2. Your friend is late to your party. He says:
   (a) Sorry you're late. (b) Sorry I'm waited.
   (c) Sorry you're waited. (d) Sorry I'm late.

3. It is exactly 2:00 now. You ate lunch at 1:30. Which expression is the best?
   (a) You ate lunch in 30 minutes. (b) You ate lunch 30 minutes ago.
   (c) You ate lunch before 30 minutes. (d) You ate lunch in 30 minutes ago.

4. Instead of saying *Donald has been married three times*, you can also say:
   (a) It's his three times. (b) It's time for three.
   (c) It's his third time. (d) It's time for third.

5. Instead of saying *Today is my 10th time to come to Disneyland*, you can also say:
   (a) I've been here 10 times. (b) I've been here 10th time.
   (c) I've been time is 10. (d) I've been time is 10th.

6. It is 10PM now. I want to go to bed at 11PM. Which expression is the best?
   (a) I'm going to bed 1 hour ago. (b) I'm going to bed 1 hour before.
   (c) I'm going to bed in 1 hour. (d) I'm going to bed in 1 hour ago.

7. If today is Monday, we can say that Wednesday is ... :
   (a) the day before yesterday (b) the day after yesterday
   (c) the day after tomorrow (d) the day before tomorrow

8. If this month is October, we can say that August was ... :
   (a) the month before next (b) the month after next
   (c) the month after last (d) the month before last

9. Imagine that today is December 23rd. Christmas Day is December 25th.
   Which answer is NOT good?
   (a) Christmas is in 2 days. (b) Christmas is in 2 days' time.
   (c) Christmas is the next day after today. (d) Christmas is the day after tomorrow.

10. Which time word (時間の関係の言葉)is not good?
    (a) the day after tomorrow (b) the week after next
    (c) the year before last (d) the month before yesterday

CHALLENGE STAGE

Challenge 3. *Did you read the English story?*
Let's check!

1.	Who was late?	*(i)*	*Yoko was late.*
		(ii)	*John was late.*
		(iii)	*Yoko and John were both late.*
		(iv)	*Nobody was late.*
2.	When did Yoko arrive?	*(i)*	*Yoko arrived 1 hour ago.*
		(ii)	*Yoko arrived 5 minutes ago.*
		(iii)	*Yoko arrived 15 minutes ago.*
		(iv)	*Yoko arrived at the same time as John.*
3.	When did John leave home?	*(i)*	*John left home an hour ago.*
		(ii)	*John left home 5 minutes ago.*
		(iii)	*John left home 4 days ago.*
		(iv)	*John left home a long time ago.*
4.	How many times has Yoko been to the café?	*(i)*	*Today is her first time.*
		(ii)	*Today is her second time.*
		(iii)	*Today is her third time.*
		(iv)	*Today is her fourth time.*
5.	When did Yoko first go to the café?	*(i)*	*She first went there 1 day ago.*
		(ii)	*She first went there 2 days ago.*
		(iii)	*She first went there 3 days ago.*
		(iv)	*She first went there 4 days ago.*
6.	Who is John meeting in 2 hours?	*(i)*	*He's meeting Paul in 2 hours.*
		(ii)	*He's meeting Ringo in 2 hours.*
		(iii)	*He's meeting Yoko in 2 hours.*
		(iv)	*He's meeting nobody in 2 hours.*
7.	When is Ringo's birthday?	*(i)*	*His birthday is in 1 day.*
		(ii)	*His birthday is in 2 days.*
		(iii)	*His birthday is in 3 days.*
		(iv)	*His birthday is in 4 days.*
8.	Where did Ringo go?	*(i)*	*He went to Japan.*
		(ii)	*He went to London.*
		(iii)	*He went to the café.*
		(iv)	*He went to John's house.*
9.	When is John's birthday?	*(i)*	*John's birthday was about 5 months ago.*
		(ii)	*John's birthday was about 3 months ago.*
		(iii)	*John's birthday was about 1 month ago.*
		(iv)	*John's birthday is in about 2 months.*
10.	When is Yoko going back to Japan?	*(i)*	*She's going back in 10 days.*
		(ii)	*She's going back in 6 days.*
		(iii)	*She's going back in 2 weeks.*
		(iv)	*She's not going back.*

"I've been waiting."

どのくらいこちらに住んでいますか？
３ヶ月住んでいます。

How long have you been living here?
I've been living here for 3 months.

QUICK START

どのくらい	どのくらい...している？	How long have you been ...?	How long
	どのくらい...している？	How long have you known...?	
	どのくらい...するつもり？	How long are you going to...?	
期間	６ヶ月間...している。	... for 6 months.	for
	長い間...している。	... for a long time.	
	３０分近く...している	... for nearly 30 minutes.	
から	金曜日から...している。	... since Friday.	since
	彼女と会ってから...している。	... since I met her.	
	学生のときから...している。	... since I was a student.	
その他	ずっと ... している。	I have been ...ing.	Other
	寂しくなる	I'll miss you.	
	現在完了進行形にできない動詞	known, seen, like etc	

You got it? (分かった？)

☺

- もう分かりましたか？
- チャレンジをやってみよう。
- *12f, 12g & 12h (ページ118~120)*にトライしよう。

- ***You got it?***
- ***Try the challenge section:***
- ***Exercises 12f, 12g, 12h (pages 118~120)***

Yes
OR
No

☹

- まだ分かりませんか？
- まず、*12b, 12c, 12d & 12e*を読んで*(ページ112~117)*
- *12f, 12g & 12h (ページ118~120)*にトライしよう。

- ***You don't get it? Not sure?***
- ***Read Sections 12b, 12c, 12d & 12e (pages 112~117)***
- ***Then, try exercises 12f, 12g, 12h (pages118~120)***

12b どのくらい

THE ENGLISH STORY

How long? - Yoko tells John why she's going back to Japan.

1 John: *I'm sorry I'm late again, Yoko. Have you been waiting long?*

2 Yoko: *I've been waiting here for nearly 30 minutes.*[1] *You're always late, John!*

3 John: *Yeah, I'm sorry Yoko. Have you really been waiting 30 minutes?*

4 Yoko: *Well ... I've been sitting here since 2 o'clock,*[2] *so I've been waiting for almost 20 minutes.*

5 John: *I'm really sorry, Yoko.*

6 Yoko: *All right, but don't do it again!*

7 John: *Okay. Umm ... Yoko ... Why are you going back to Japan?*

8 Yoko: *My sister's getting married. I have to go back for the wedding.*

9 John: *But Yoko, how long have you been living here?*[3] *Two months?*

10 Yoko: *I've been living here for nearly 3 months.*

11 John: *Only 3 months? How long have we known each other?*[4]

12 Yoko: *Umm ... let me see ... I've known you for almost 8 weeks.*

13 John: *How long are you going to stay in Japan?*[5]

14 Yoko: *I'm staying for a long time. I'm not coming back here.*

15 John: *But Yoko, what are you going to do back in Japan?*

16 Yoko: *I want to be an English teacher. I've been studying English here.*

17 John: *I didn't know that. How long have you been studying here?*

18 Yoko: *I've been studying English here since I came.*

19 John: *Yoko ... Yoko ... Umm ... please don't go! I'll miss you!*[6]

20 Yoko: *I'm sorry John, but I have to go back.*

THE JAPANESE STORY

12c どのくらい

どのくらい？ - ヨーコはジョンに日本に帰る理由を伝えます。

1 ジョン： ヨーコ、ごめん。また遅れちゃった。だいぶ待った？

2 ヨーコ： 私は、ここで３０分近く待っているわ。[1] ジョンはいつも遅刻するんだから！

3 ジョン： ああ、ごめんよ、ヨーコ。ほんとうに３０分も待ったの？

4 ヨーコ： そうね … ２時からずっとここに座っているわ。[2] ほとんど２０分待っているわ。

5 ジョン： ほんとうにごめんなさい、ヨーコ。

6 ヨーコ： いいわよ。でももうしないでね。

7 ジョン： わかったよ。あの … ヨーコ … どうして日本に帰るの？

8 ヨーコ： 姉が結婚するのよ。結婚式のために帰らなきゃならないの。

9 ジョン： でもヨーコ、君はどのくらいここに住んでいるの？[3] ２ヶ月？

10 ヨーコ： ３ヶ月近くになるわ。

11 ジョン： たった３ヶ月かい？ 僕らが知り合ってどのくらいになる？[4]

12 ヨーコ： そうねぇ … ええと … ８週間くらいになるわ。

13 ジョン： どのくらい日本にいるつもりなの？[5]

14 ヨーコ： ずっとよ。ここには戻って来ないわ。

15 ジョン： でもヨーコ、日本に帰って何をするつもりなの？

16 ヨーコ： 英語の先生になりたいのよ。ここで英語を勉強していたの。

17 ジョン： 知らなかったよ。ここでどのくらい勉強しているの？

18 ヨーコ： ここに来てからずっとよ。

19 ジョン： ヨーコ … あのさ … 行かないで欲しいんだ。寂しくなるよ。[6]

20 ヨーコ： ジョン、ごめんね。でも帰らなきゃならないの。

A: How long have you been driving taxis?
B: I've been driving taxis for 10 years.

A: タクシーの運転をいつからやってるの？
B: 10年間、タクシーの運転をしています。

* * *

A: How long has he been living in Rome?
B: He's been living there since 1990.

A: 彼はローマにいつから住んでいますか？
B: 彼は1990年からあそこに住んでいます。

* * *

A: How long has she been teaching?
B: She's been teaching since she was 22.

A: いつから彼女は教えていますか？
B: 彼女は２２歳の時から教えています。

* * *

A: How long has he been smoking?
B: He's been smoking since high school.

A: 彼はいつから喫煙していますか？
B: 彼は高校時代から喫煙しています。

* * *

A: How long are you staying in Los Angeles?
B: I'm staying for about 5 days.

A: どのくらいの間ロスに滞在するつもりですか？
B: ５日間くらい滞在する予定です。

* * *

A: How long is he going to live here?
B: He's going to live here for 2 years.

A: 彼はどのくらいの間ここに住むつもりですか？
B: 彼は２年間ここに住むつもりです。

* * *

A: How long's he gonna work in Osaka?
B: He's gonna work there for 6 weeks.

A: 彼はどのくらいの間大阪で働くつもりですか？
B: 6週間仕事をするつもりです。

* * *

A: How long have you known him?
B: I've known him for 3 years.

A: 彼と知り合ってどのくらいですか？
B: 彼と知り合ってから、3年間になります。

* * *

A: How long's she had short hair?
B: She's had short hair since May.

A: 彼女はいつから短い髪にしているの？
B: 彼女は５月から短い髪にしています。

LEARN THESE SENTENCES

12e
どのくらい

1　３０分待っている。 I've been waiting for 30 minutes.

Look at the diagram. Do you understand?

キーワード		標準英語		会話的
for	→	How long have you been waiting?	→	*I've been waiting* ***for*** *3 hours.* *I've been waiting* ***for*** *8 days.* *I've been waiting* ***for*** *20 minutes.*

What's wrong?
I've been waiting for 3 hours!

書いてある例は全部 have been ...ing の文だけど、他にも色々あるよ。あとでね。

	日本語		英語
例１	私は、１２時間以上ずっと勉強している。	→	*I've been studying for over 12 hours.*
例２	２日間ずっと雨が降っています。	→	*It's been raining for two days.*
例３	彼女は２０年以上ずっと煙草を吸っています。	→	*She's been smoking for over 20 years.*

I've been working as a chef for 25 years.

→

2　２時から座ってる。 I've been sitting here since 2.

Look at the diagram. Do you understand?

キーワード		標準英語		会話的
since	→	How long have you been waiting?	→	*I've been waiting* ***since*** *2 o'clock.* *I've been waiting* ***since*** *lunchtime.* *I've been waiting* ***since*** *I arrived.*

We've been drinking since 3 o'clock.

	日本語		英語
例１	昼の３時からずっと寝ています。	→	*I've been sleeping* ***since*** *3PM.*
例２	昨日からずっと雨が降っています。	→	*It's been raining* ***since*** *yesterday.*
例３	彼女は１６才からずっと煙草を吸っています。	→	*She's been smoking* ***since*** *she was 16.*
まとめ	私は1987年から30年以上日本に住んでいます。	→	*I've been living in Japan* ***since*** *1987,* ***for*** *over 30 years.*

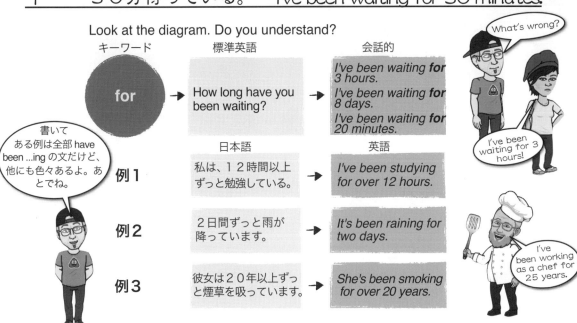

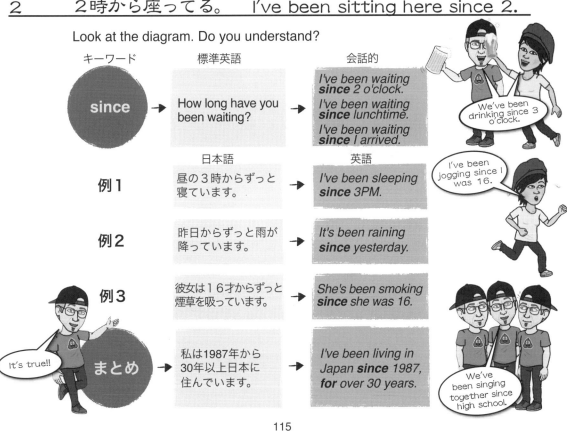

I've been jogging since I was 16.

It's true!!

We've been singing together since high school.

LEARN THESE SENTENCES

3 　どのくらい … している？ 　How long have you been ...

Look at the diagram. Do you understand?

キーワード 　　　　基本モデル

どのくらい

How long
have you been

→

waiting? studying?	(動詞)
a teacher a student	(名詞)
sleepy busy	(形容詞)

How long have we been dating?

We've been dating for 2 months!

日本語 　　　　　英語

例1
(動詞)

どのくらいサッカー
をしていますか？
→
*How long **have** you **been** playing soccer?*

例2
(動詞)

彼女はパリにどのくら
い住んでいますか？
→
*How long **has** she **been** living in Paris?*

例3
(動詞)

どのくらい雪が降っ
ていますか？
→
*How long **has** it **been** snowing?*

例4
(名詞)

どのくらい歌手をし
ていますか？
→
*How long **have** you **been a singer**?*

例5
(形容詞)

彼女はどのくらいそん
なに忙しくしている
の？
→
*How long **has** she **been** so busy?*

How long have you been a singer?

How long have you been a cook?

4 　どのくらい … している？ 　How long have you ...

Look at the diagram. Do you understand?

キーワード 　　　基本モデル 　　　特別な動詞

*書いてある
動詞を覚えてお
いてね。*

どのくらい

How long have you

→

***known** her?*
***liked** beer?*
***had** a dog?*
***belonged** to the gym?*

How long have you belonged to the gym?

I joined yesterday.

日本語 　　　　　英語

例

どのくらい風邪を引
いているの？
→
*How long **have** you **had a cold**?*

have been ...ing
出来ない動詞

見る、好き、愛する、
持つ、所属する、理解
する、分かる
→
see, like, love, have belong, understand, know

How long have I loved beer?

That's a good question...

12e

どのくらい

LEARN THESE SENTENCES

5　どのくらい...つもりですか？ How long are you going to...

Look at the diagram. Do you understand?

キーワード

どのくらい
(未来)

忘れずに。How long are you going to ... と How long are you ...ing は同じだよ。後の方はとても会話的だよ。

gonna は かっこいいけど、俗語だよ。あまり丁寧じゃない,,,

基本モデル

How long are you going to

How long (are) you gonna

 → stay there?
live in Canada?
study tonight?
be in Sapporo?

	日本語		英語
例1 (普通)	どのくらいロスに滞在するつもりですか？	→	*How long **are you going to** stay in LA?*
例2 (俗語)	どのくらい(の間)ロスにいるの？	→	*How long **(are) you gonna** stay in LA?*
例3 (会話的)	どのくらい(の間)ロスに滞在するつもり？	→	*How long **(are) you staying** in LA?*
例4	今晩、どのくらい働くの？	→	*How long **are you gonna** work tonight?*
	真夜中まで働くつもりだ。		*I'm working until midnight.*
例5	どのくらい寝るつもりですか？	→	*How long **are you going to** sleep?*
	起きるまで寝るつもりです。		*I'm going to sleep until I wake up!*

How long are you working tonight?

I get off at 7PM. Wanna meet?

How long are you gonna stay in Japan?

I'm gonna stay there forever!

6　寂しくなります。　　I'll miss you.

Look at the diagram. Do you get it?

標準日本語

寂しくなる。

I'll miss you.「淋しくなります」という意味だよ。

標準英語		会話的
I will miss you.	→	*I'll miss you.* *Miss you.*

日本語		英語
もう行かなくちゃ。さよなら。寂しいよね。	→	*I have to go now.* *Bye. I'll miss you.*
寂しいよ！さようなら！		*I'll miss you too.* *G'bye!*

Yoko. Don't go. I'll miss you.

Sorry John, but I have to go.

CHALLENGE STAGE

Challenge 1. *Fill in the blanks from the list.*

1	Charles:	I'm sorry I'm late, Di. ずいぶん待ったの？
2	Di:	１時間も待っています！ You're always late Charles!
3	Charles:	Yeah, I'm sorry Di. ほんとうに１時間待ったの？
4	Di:	Well, I've been sitting here since 4 o'clock, so I've been waiting for almost 50 minutes.
5	Charles:	ほんとうにごめんなさい、ダイ。
6	Di:	All right, but don't do it again!
7	Charles:	Okay. Anyway Di, how long have we known each other?
8	Di:	私たちが知り合ってから１５年になります。
9	Charles:	I see. How long have we been married?
10	Di:	私たちが結婚してから１０年以上になります。
11	Charles:	And how long have you been a mother?
12	Di:	私が母親になってから１０年になります。
13	Charles:	And how long have we been fighting with each other?
14	Di:	私たちは結婚してからずっとけんかをしています。
15	Charles:	So why did we get married, Di?
16	Di:	That's a very good question!

Choose the best sentence for the blanks:

a) I've been a mother for 10 years.
b) I'm really sorry, Di.
c) I've been waiting for an hour!
d) We've been fighting with each other since we got married.
e) Have you been waiting long?
f) We've been married for over 10 years.
g) We've known each other for 15 years.
h) Have you really been waiting an hour?

CHALLENGE STAGE

Challenge 2. *Circle the correct answer.*

1. Clarke gets home 30 minutes late. What does Lois say?
   (a) I've been waiting since 30 minutes. (b) I've been waiting for 30 minutes.
   (c) I've been waited since 30 minutes. (d) I've been waited for 30 minutes.

2. Today is Sunday. It started raining on Friday.
   (a) It has been raining for Friday. (b) It has been raining for Sunday.
   (c) It has been raining since Sunday. (d) It has been raining since Friday.

3. Alán began driving when he was 16. Which answer is best?
   (a) Alán has been driving for 16. (b) Alán has been driving since he was 16.
   (c) Alán has been driving for he is 16. (d) Alán has been drive since 16.

4. Which sentence is best?
   (a) Jack have been a baker for a year. (b) Jack have been a baker since a year.
   (c) Jack has been a baker for a year. (d) Jack has been a baker since a year.

5. The answer is *I've been smoking since I was 18.* What is the question?
   (a) How long are you smoking? (b) How long did you smoke?
   (c) How long have you smoke? (d) How long have you been smoking?

6. Which sentence is NOT good?
   (a) I have been knowing him since May. (b) I have been watching her since June.
   (c) I have been working since July. (d) I have been jogging since August.

7. I have got a bad cold so I went to the doctor. He said;
   (a) How long have you had a cold? (b) How long have you been having a cold?
   (c) How long did you have a cold? (d) How long have you been cold?

8. Which question is the SAME as *How long is he going to stay here*?
   (a) How long is he staying here? (b) How long did he stay here?
   (c) How long has he stayed here? (d) How long has he been staying here?

9. The question is *How long are you gonna work in Tokyo*? The best answer is;
   (a) I've been working there for 2 years. (b) I have worked there for 2 years.
   (c) I'm going to work there for 2 years. (d) I'm gonna working there for 2 years.

10. Keith is going to USA. Mick is staying in England. Mick will be lonely. What does he say?
   (a) Please don't go. I'll miss you. (b) Please don't go. I'll miss me.
   (c) Please don't go. You'll miss you. (d) Please don't go. I'll misuse.

CHALLENGE STAGE

Challenge 3. Did you read the English story?
Let's check!

1. Why is John sorry?
   - *(i)* *Because he forgot Yoko's name.*
   - *(ii)* *Because he forgot Yoko.*
   - *(iii)* *Because he is early.*
   - *(iv)* *Because he is late.*

2. How long was Yoko waiting?
   - *(i)* *She was waiting for 30 seconds.*
   - *(ii)* *She was waiting for 30 minutes.*
   - *(iii)* *She was waiting for 30 hours.*
   - *(iv)* *She was waiting for 30 days.*

3. Yoko says that John is always;
   - *(i)* *handsome.*
   - *(ii)* *late.*
   - *(iii)* *interesting.*
   - *(iv)* *lonely.*

4. How long has Yoko been sitting there?
   - *(i)* *She's been sitting there since 2 o'clock.*
   - *(ii)* *She's been sitting there since 2:30.*
   - *(iii)* *She's been sitting there since 3 o'clock.*
   - *(iv)* *She's been sitting there since 3:30.*

5. Why is Yoko going back to Japan?
   - *(i)* *Because she has to work.*
   - *(ii)* *Because she has to study.*
   - *(iii)* *Because her sister is getting married.*
   - *(iv)* *Because she likes Japan.*

6. How long have Yoko and John known each other?
   - *(i)* *They have known each other for 4 weeks.*
   - *(ii)* *They have known each other for 6 weeks.*
   - *(iii)* *They have known each other for 8 weeks.*
   - *(iv)* *They have known each other for 10 weeks.*

7. How long has Yoko been in Australia?
   - *(i)* *She's been there for nearly 2 months.*
   - *(ii)* *She's been there for nearly 3 months.*
   - *(iii)* *She's been there for nearly 6 months.*
   - *(iv)* *She's been there for nearly 8 months.*

8. How long is Yoko going to stay in Japan?
   - *(i)* *She's staying in Japan for 2 months.*
   - *(ii)* *She's staying in Japan for 8 months.*
   - *(iii)* *She's staying in Japan for 2 years.*
   - *(iv)* *She's staying in Japan for a long time.*

9. What does Yoko want to do in Japan?
   - *(i)* *She wants to be a pop star.*
   - *(ii)* *She wants to be a cafe owner.*
   - *(iii)* *She wants to be a dancer.*
   - *(iv)* *She wants to be an English teacher.*

10. How long has Yoko been studying English?
    - *(i)* *She's been studying for 20 minutes.*
    - *(ii)* *She's been studying since 2 o'clock.*
    - *(iii)* *She's been studying since she came.*
    - *(iv)* *She's been studying since John came.*

"Gotta go!"

QUICK START

しなければ	僕は行かなければならない。（等）	*I have to go.*	has got to
	僕は行かなければならない。	*I must go.*	
	僕は行かなければならない。	*I have got to go.*	
	僕は行かなければならない。	*I need to go.*	
するべき	僕は行くべき／行った方が良いです。	*I should go.*	should
	僕は行くべき／行った方が良いです。	*I'd better go.*	
	僕は行くべき／行った方が良いです。	*I ought to go.*	
省略	行かなくちゃ。	*I gotta go.*	abbreviations
	行かなきゃ。	*I hafta go.*	
	行った方がいい。	*I oughta go.*	
	行かなくていい。	*I don't hafta go.*	
その他	行かなくても良いです。	*You don't have to go.*	Other
	行ってはいけません。	*You must not go.*	
	...と思いますか？	*Do you think ...?*	

You got it? (分かった？)

☺

・もう分かりましたか？
・チャレンジをやってみよう。
・*13f, 13g & 13h (ページ128~130)*にトライしよう。

・***You got it?***
・***Try the challenge section:***
・***Exercises 13f, 13g, 13h (pages 128~130)***

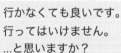

☹

・まだ分かりませんか？
・まず、*13b, 13c, 13d & 13e*を読んで*(ページ122~127)*
・*13f, 13g & 13h (ページ128~130)*にトライしよう。

・***You don't get it? Not sure?***
・***Read Sections 13b, 13c, 13d & 13e (pages 122~127)***
・***Then, try exercises 13f, 13g, 13h (pages128~130)***

13b
提案

THE ENGLISH STORY

Suggestions - Paul and John discuss Yoko's farewell party.

1 Paul: *Hi John. How' you doing?*

2 John: *Not so good, Paul. I'm kinda' sad because Yoko's leaving soon.*

3 Paul: *Yeah? I didn't know that. Why is she leaving?*

4 John: *She's got to go back to Japan*[1] *for her sister's wedding.*

5 Paul: *That's too bad, John. You really like her, don't you?*

6 John: *Yeah, I guess so.*

7 Paul: *Heh! I've got an idea! Let's have a farewell party for her!*

8 John: *Good idea. Who should we invite?*[2]

9 Paul: *That's a good question. You know most of her friends, don't you?*

10 John: *Yeah. Let me see ... we can invite Ringo and George and ...*

11 Paul: *Do you think we ought to invite Alcindo?*[3]

12 John: *Okay. Yoko likes soccer. We'd better invite Kazu, too.*[4]

13 Paul: *Mm ... What about Mick and Keith? Do we have to invite them?*[5]

14 John: *No, we don't have to invite them.*[6]

15 Paul: *Do we need to invite Arnie?*[7]

16 John: *Arnie? Who's Arnie?*

17 Paul: *You know ... Arnie ... the German guy.*

18 John: *Oh! Big Arnie! Yeah, we must invite Arnie.*[8] *Um ... He went to America, didn't he?*

19 Paul: *Yeah, but he'll be back. Ahhh ... What about Michael J?*

20 John: *No way! Please!! You must not invite him!*[9]

21 Paul: *All right. But we gotta invite Jake.*[10]

22 John: *And if we invite Jake, we oughta invite Elwood.*[11]

23 Paul: *Okay. I think this party will be really great!*

24 John: *Yeah, but I wish Yoko wasn't going back to Japan.*

THE JAPANESE STORY

提案 - ポールとジョンはヨーコの送別会について話します。

1 ポール: やあ、ジョン。調子はどうだい？

2 ジョン: あまりよくないよ、ポール。ヨーコがいなくなるから、何だか寂しくて。

3 ポール: そうなのか？ 知らなかったよ。彼女はどうしていなくなるんだい？

4 ジョン: お姉さんの結婚式があるんだよ。そのために帰らなくちゃならないんだ。[1]

5 ポール: それは残念だなあ。君はほんとうに彼女のことが好きなんだろう？

6 ジョン: うん、そう思う。

7 ポール: おい、いい考えがあるぞ。彼女のお別れパーティーをしよう！

8 ジョン: グッド・アイディアだ。誰を誘えばいいだろう？[2]

9 ポール: それはいい質問だな。君は彼女の友達をほとんど知ってるんだろう？

10 ジョン: ああ。そうだなあ ... リンゴとジョージを誘って ...

11 ポール: アルシンドも誘った方がいいと思うかい？[3]

12 ジョン: オーケー。ヨーコはサッカーが好きだ。カズも呼んだ方がいいだろう。[4]

13 ポール: うーん ... ミックとキースは？ あいつらも誘わないといけないの？[5]

14 ジョン: いいや、彼らは誘わなくていいよ。[6]

15 ポール: アーニーを呼ばないとだめかい？[7]

16 ジョン: アーニー？ アーニーって誰だ？

17 ポール: ほら ... アーニーだよ。ドイツの奴さ。

18 ジョン: ああ！「巨漢のアーニー」だな！うん、アーニーは呼ばないとだめだ。[8]
ええと ... あいつはアメリカに行ったよね？

19 ポール: ああ、でも戻ってくるよ。あのさー ... マイケル・Jはどうする？

20 ジョン: やめてくれよ！ 頼むよ！！ あいつは誘ったらダメだ！[9]

21 ポール: わかったよ。でもジェイクを呼ばなきゃだめだな。[10]

22 ジョン: もしジェイクを呼ぶんだったら、エルウッドも誘った方が良いよね。[11]

23 ポール: オーケー。すごいパーティーになりそうだな。

24 ジョン: ああ、でもヨーコが日本になんて帰らなければいいのに ...

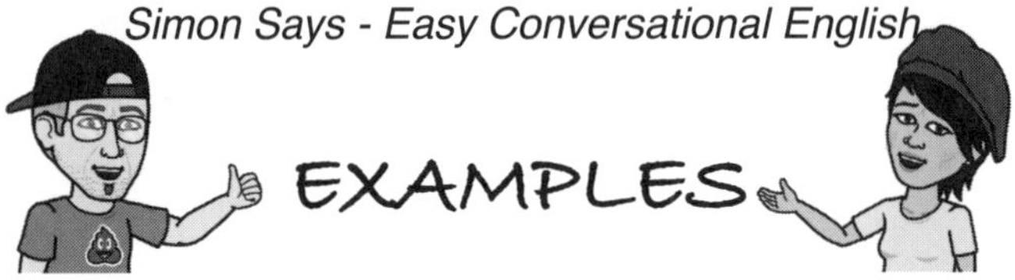

A: *Do vampires have to drink blood?*
B: *Yes, they have to.*

A: 吸血鬼は血を吸わないとだめなの？
B: うん。そうしないとだめです。

* * *

A: *Have I got to wear clothes?*
B: *Yes Tarzan, you've got to.*

A: 服を着ないとだめですか？
B: そうターザン。着なければなりません。

* * *

A: *Must zombies chase people?*
B: *Yes, they must.*

A: ゾンビは人を追いかけないとだめですか？
B: そうですね。しないとだめです。

* * *

A: *Should we fix the pipe?*
B: *Yes Mario, we'd better fix it.*

A: パイプを直した方が良い？
B: そうだよマリオ。直した方が良いです。

* * *

A: *Do you think I ought to quit.*
B: *Yes Donald. You ought to quit.*

A: （仕事を）やめた方が良いと思いますか？
B: そうですよドナルド。やめた方がいいよ。

* * *

A: *Can I touch the lion, Mummy?*
B: *No! You must not touch him!*

A: ねえママ、ライオンさんに触っていい？
B: だめですよ。絶対に触っちゃだめ。

* * *

A: *Do I have to go to school?*
B: *No Steve. You don't have to.*

A: 学校に行かなければならないの？
B: いいえスティーブ、行かなくていいですよ。

* * *

A: *What time does Santa come?*
B: *He oughta be here soon.*

A: サンタさんは、何時に来るの？
B: もう少しで来るはずだよ。

* * *

A: *Let's go drinking!*
B: *It's kinda late. I hafta go home.*

A: 飲みに行こうよ！
B: もう遅いよ。もう帰らなくちゃ。

* * *

A: *It's almost midnight!*
B: *Midnight? I gotta go!*

A: もう少しで真夜中（１２時）だよ。
B: １２時？ もう行かなくちゃ。

LEARN THESE SENTENCES

13e
提案

1　帰らなければならない。 She's got to go back.

（説明は一緒）

5 Do we have to invite them?
7 Do we need to invite Arnie?
8 We must invite Arnie.

To make an omelette, you must break eggs.

Look at the diagram. Do you understand?

ポイント		英語		文章
しなければならない	→	has/have got to has/have to need/needs to must	→	*She's **got to** go back.* *We **have to** invite him.* *I **need to** call her.* *You **must** listen to me.*

	日本語		英語
例1	新しいコンピューターを買わないと。	→	*I've **got** to buy a new computer.*
例2	日曜日までにレポートを書かなければならない。	→	*We **have to** write a report by Sunday.*
例3	私は、息子と話さないとだめですね。	→	*I **need to** talk to my son.*
例4	果物と野菜を食べなければなりません。	→	*You **must** eat fruit and vegetables.*
疑問文1	あなたは、今行かないとだめですか？	→	*Do you **have to** go now?*
疑問文2	彼女は、病院に行かなければならないの？	→	***Has** she **got to** go to hospital?*

I need to drink my medicine.

You wanna eat out with me tonight?
Yeah, but I have to change my clothes.

2　誰を呼べばいいだろう？ Who should we invite?

（説明は一緒）

3 Do you think we ought to invite Alcindo?
4 We'd better invite Kazu, too?

Look at the diagram. Do you understand?

ポイント		英語		文章
するべき（した方が良い）	→	should had better ought to	→	*Who **should** we invite?* *You'**d better** go to bed.* *He **ought to** get a job.*

提案

LEARN THESE SENTENCES

should はhad better やought to と同じ意味だよ。でも、疑問文を作るときは、should を使うのが一番いいよ。

John, you should stop drinking!

Yoko, you should stop shopping!

	日本語		英語
例1	明日は、暖かいはずです。	→	It **should** be warm tomorrow.
例2	お医者さんを呼んだ方が良いよ。	→	You**'d better** call the doctor.
例3	彼女は貯金するべきだ。	→	She **ought to** save her money.
疑問文	俺は留まるべきか、進むべきか？	→	**Should** I stay or **should** I go now?

3　　…した方が良いと思う？　Do you think we should…

Look at the diagram. Do you understand?

ポイント	英語	文章	
? するべき (した方が良い)	should had better ought to	**Should** I go? **Had** I **better** go? **Ought** I **to** go?	O X X

Do you think I should wear a dress?

No. You look great in jeans.

	日本語		英語
疑問文1	彼女に電話した方が良いですか？	O	**Should** I call her?
疑問文2	彼女に電話した方が良いですか？	X	**Had** I **better** call her?
疑問文3	彼女に電話した方が良いですか？	X	**Ought** I to **call** her?
疑問文4	彼女に電話した方が良いと思いますか？	O	**Do you think** I should call her?
疑問文5	彼女に電話した方が良いと思いますか？	O	**Do you think** I'd better call her?
疑問文6	彼女に電話した方が良いと思いますか？	O	**Do you think** I ought to call her?

had better や ought to の疑問文は、文法的には正しいけれど、聞いていると少し変な感じがするよ。

Do you think I ought to call her?

Yeah, I think you should.

LEARN THESE SENTENCES

6 ...しなくていいよ。 We don't have to ...

Look at the diagram. Do you understand?

ポイント	英語	文章
しなくていい	don't/doesn't have to →	*You **don't have to** go.* *I **don't have to** eat.* *She **doesn't have to** pay.*

	日本語	英語
例	我々は説明しなくていいよ。 →	*We **don't have** to explain.*

I don't wanna go!

No problem. You don't have to go.

8 ...してはだめです。 We must not ...

Look at the diagram. Do you understand?

ポイント	英語	文章
してはだめ	must not →	*You **must not** smoke!* *He **mustn't** speak.* *She **must not** laugh.*

	日本語	英語
例	運転中、携帯を使ってはだめです。 →	*You **mustn't** use your phone while driving.*

You mustn't carry a big knife!

10 ...を誘わなくちゃ... We gotta invite ...

(説明は一緒) 11 We oughta invite Elwood.

これはフォーマルな表現じゃないよ。友達同士だけに使って、フォーマルの場では使わないでね。

Look at the diagram. Do you understand?

標準日本語	標準英語	会話的
省略	have got to have to ought to don't have to →	***gotta*** ***hafta*** ***oughta*** ***don't hafta***

	日本語	英語
例1	行かなくちゃ。 →	*I **gotta** go.*
例2	食べなくちゃ。 →	*We **hafta** eat!*
例3	勉強するべきだ！ →	*You **oughta** study.*

Cool T shirt. You look great!

I don't like it.

I gotta buy a new one.

I hafta go shopping NOW!

13f
提案

CHALLENGE STAGE

Challenge 1. *Fill in the blanks from the list.*

1	Ginger:	Hey Fred, I've got an idea! Let's have a party!
2	Fred:	Good idea. 誰を誘えばいいですか？
3	Ginger:	That's a good question!
4	Fred:	チャーリーを誘った方がいいと思いますよ。
5	Ginger:	Yeah, we'd better invite Charlie. What about Clarke?
6	Fred:	クラークも誘った方がいいですよ。Should we invite Vivian?
7	Ginger:	もちろん！ビビアンも誘った方がいいですよ。
8	Fred:	What about Gary?
9	Ginger:	ギャリーは誘わなくても良いです。
10	Fred:	Okay. Do we need to invite Marlene?
11	Ginger:	マリーンって誰ですか？
12	Fred:	You know ... Marlene ... the German girl.
13	Ginger:	Oh! Marlene! マリーンは誘わなくていけません。
14	Fred:	Do you think we ought to invite Errol?
15	Ginger:	エロルは絶対に誘ってはいけません。
16	Fred:	All right. I think this party will be really great!

Choose the best sentence for the blanks:

a) Who's Marlene?

b) No way! We must not invite Errol.

c) Yeah, we ought to invite Clarke.

d) Of course! We'd better invite Vivian.

e) Who should we invite?

f) I think we should invite Charlie.

g) We don't have to invite Gary.

h) We must invite Marlene!

CHALLENGE STAGE

Challenge 2. *Circle the correct answer.*

1. Which expression (表現) does NOT mean the same as *You must study everyday*?
   (a) You have to study everyday.
   (b) You have got to study everyday.
   (c) You ought to study everyday.
   (d) You've got to study everyday.

2. The expression *Freddie must go to the opera* is the same as:
   (a) Freddie should go to the opera.
   (b) Freddie has to go to the opera.
   (c) Freddie must not go to the opera.
   (d) Freddie might go to the opera.

3. The expression *We need to sleep* is the same as:
   (a) We don't have to sleep.
   (b) We have got to sleep.
   (c) We had better sleep.
   (d) We must not sleep.

4. Which 3 words (or word combinations) are the same?
   (a) have to, have got to, need to
   (b) have got to, had better, ought to
   (c) need to, have to, had better
   (d) have got to, should, had better

5. The expression *You should eat 3 times a day* is the same as:
   (a) You've got to eat 3 times a day.
   (b) You don't have to eat 3 times a day.
   (c) You mustn't eat 3 times a day.
   (d) You ought to eat 3 times a day.

6. Which is the best conversational question?
   (a) Hadn't you better get up early?
   (b) Ought you to get up early?
   (c) Must you not get up early?
   (d) Should you get up early?

7. Which is the best question?
   (a) Do you think we ought to go?
   (b) Do you think we'd better go?
   (c) Do you think we should go?
   (d) All sentences are okay.

8. Which 3 words (or word combinations) are the same?
   (a) ought to, should, must
   (b) had better, have got to, should
   (c) should, must, have got to
   (d) had better, should, ought to

9. Which sentence means *It is wrong to cheat* (カンニングする)?
   (a) You don't have to cheat.
   (b) You had better cheat.
   (c) You must not cheat.
   (d) You have got to cheat.

10. In very colloquial English (口語), what can you say instead of *I have got to sleep?*
   (a) I got sleep.
   (b) I gotta sleep.
   (c) I get sleep.
   (d) I don't gotta sleep.

13h
提案

CHALLENGE STAGE

Challenge 3. *Did you read the English story?*
Let's check!

1. Why is John sad?
   - *(i) He's sad because he spent his money.*
   - *(ii) He's sad because he lost his phone.*
   - *(iii) He's sad because Yoko's leaving.*
   - *(iv) He's sad because he hates parties.*

2. Why is Yoko leaving?
   - *(i) She has to go to her sister's wedding.*
   - *(ii) She has to go to school.*
   - *(iii) She has to start working.*
   - *(iv) She has no more money.*

3. What is Paul's idea?
   - *(i) Paul wants to have a farewell party.*
   - *(ii) Paul wants to go to Japan with Yoko.*
   - *(iii) Paul wants to tell Yoko to stay.*
   - *(iv) Paul wants to go drinking with John.*

4. What sport does Yoko like?
   - *(i) She likes darts.*
   - *(ii) She likes badminton.*
   - *(iii) She likes softball.*
   - *(iv) She likes soccer.*

5. What is the German guy's name?
   - *(i) His name is Andrew.*
   - *(ii) His name is Albert.*
   - *(iii) His name is Adolph.*
   - *(iv) His name is Arnie.*

6. Where did Arnie go?
   - *(i) He went to America.*
   - *(ii) He went to Germany.*
   - *(iii) He went to Tokyo.*
   - *(iv) He went to John's house.*

7. Who mustn't Paul invite?
   - *(i) He mustn't invite Michael J.*
   - *(ii) He mustn't invite Mick.*
   - *(iii) He mustn't invite Keith.*
   - *(iv) He mustn't invite Kazu.*

8. If Paul invites Jake, he also has to invite
   - *(i) Michael J.*
   - *(ii) Ringo.*
   - *(iii) Elwood.*
   - *(iv) George.*

9. What does Paul say about the party?
   - *(i) He says the party will be really good.*
   - *(ii) He says the party will be really bad.*
   - *(iii) He says the party will be really noisy.*
   - *(iv) He says the party will be really strange.*

10. What does John wish?
    - *(i) He wishes Yoko wasn't going to Japan.*
    - *(ii) He wishes Yoko liked him.*
    - *(iii) He wishes Yoko gave him money.*
    - *(iv) He wishes he could go to Japan.*

"Take care!"

14a
別れ

QUICK START

 感謝

来てくれてありがとう。	*Thanks for coming.*	
ピザをありがとう。	*Thanks for the pizza.*	**Thanks**

関係代名詞

...をしている男です。	*He's the guy that ...*	
...をしている女です。	*She's the woman that ...*	**...that...**
...をしている人です。	*He's the one that ...*	

２０代前半後半

彼女は２０代前半です。	*She's in her early 20s.*	
彼は３０代半ばです。	*He's in his mid 30s.*	***early/late 20s***
僕は４０代後半です。	*I'm in my late 40s.*	

その他

...のことですか？	*You mean ...?*	
連絡してね。	*Keep in touch.*	**Other**
気をつけてください。	*Take care.*	

You got it? (分かった？)

☺

 Yes OR No

☹

・もう分かりましたか？
・チャレンジをやってみよう。
・*14f, 14g & 14h (ページ138~140)* にトライしよう。

・You got it?
・*Try the challenge section:*
・*Exercises 14f, 14g, 14h (pages 138~140)*

・まだ分かりませんか？
・まず、*14b, 14c, 14d & 14e* を読んで(ページ132~137)
・*14f, 14g & 14h (ページ138~140)* にトライしよう。

・*You don't get it? Not sure?*
・*Read Sections 14b, 14c, 14d & 14e (pages 132~137)*
・*Then, try exercises 14f, 14g, 14h (pages138~140)*

14b 別れ

THE ENGLISH STORY

Parting - John has a farewell party for Yoko.

1 Yoko: *Hey John! This is a really great party! Thanks for inviting everyone.*[1]

2 John: *That's okay Yoko. By the way, there are one or two people here that I don't know.*

3 Yoko: *Who?*

4 John: *Well, who's that guy over there?*

5 Yoko: *You mean Ron?*[2] *He's the guy that I go mountain biking with.*[3]

6 John: *Oh, I see. And who's that ... the guy with the backpack?*

7 Yoko: *Oh, that's Glenn. He's the guy that I go climbing with.*

8 John: *Okay. How about the short guy with no hair?*

9 Yoko: *That's Brick. He's the one that I work-out with at the gym.*

10 John: *Who is the guy next to him?*

11 Yoko: *That's Franklin. He's the guy that teaches me aerobics.*

12 John: *And who's the lady that's standing in the kitchen?*

13 Yoko: *That's Wendy. She's the girl that I met at Al's Bar.*

14 John: *She looks young. How old is she?*

15 Yoko: *She's in her early 30s.*[4]

16 John: *Uh huh. I think I know everyone else.*

17 Yoko: *I really don't want to leave, but I've gotta' go back. Sorry John.*

18 John: *That's okay Yoko. Keep in touch,*[5] *okay?*

19 Yoko: *Okay, I'll email you.*

20 John: *And take care of yourself.*[6]

21 Yoko: *You too, John. Thanks for everything.*

22 John: *No problem Yoko. Goodbye and good luck.*

THE JAPANESE STORY

14c
別れ

別れ - ジョンはヨーコの送別会を開きます。

1 ヨーコ: ねえ、ジョン！とても立派なパーティーだわ。皆を招待してくれてありがとう。[1]

2 ジョン: いいんだ、ヨーコ。ところで、ひとりかふたり、僕の知らない人がいるんだけど。

3 ヨーコ: 誰？

4 ジョン: あのさ、あそこにいる（男の）人は誰だい？

5 ヨーコ: ロンのこと？[2] 彼とはマウンテン・バイクにいっしょに行ったの。[3]

6 ジョン: ああ、わかった。それとあの人は ... バックパックを背負った人は？

7 ヨーコ: ああ、あれはグレンよ。彼とは一緒に登山に行ったの。

8 ジョン: オーケー。あの背が低くて髪がない人は？

9 ヨーコ: ブリックよ。彼とはジムで一緒にトレーニングしたの。

10 ジョン: 彼の隣の奴は誰だい？

11 ヨーコ: フランクリンよ。私にエアロビクスを教えてくれたの。

12 ジョン: キッチンに立っている女の人は誰？

13 ヨーコ: ウェンディーよ。アルズ・バーで会ったの。

14 ジョン: 彼女は若く見えるけど、何歳だろうか？

15 ヨーコ: 彼女は３０代前半ですよ。[4]

16 ジョン: なるほど。全員わかったと思うよ。

17 ヨーコ: ほんとうは行きたくないの。でも行かなくちゃならないのよ。ジョン、ごめんね。

18 ジョン: いいよヨーコ。連絡してね、[5] いいかい？

19 ヨーコ: ええ、メールを送るわ。

20 ジョン: それから身体に気をつけて。[6]

21 ヨーコ: ジョン、あなたもね。何もかもありがとう。

22 ジョン: 気にしないで、ヨーコ。さようなら。頑張ってね。

EXAMPLES

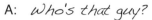

A: *Who's that guy?*
B: *You mean Phil? He's the guy that I play darts with.*

*　　*　　*

A: *Who's that lady?*
B: *She's the girl that Glenn is dating.*

*　　*　　*

A: *Who's the short lady with the cute face?*
B: *You mean Suzy? She's the girl that I told you about.*

*　　*　　*

A: *How old is that girl?*
B: *Betty? She's in her early 20s.*

*　　*　　*

A: *Thanks for the beer!*
B: *That's okay.*

*　　*　　*

A: *Thanks for teaching me this year.*
B: *No problem.*

*　　*　　*

A: *I have to go now. Bye!!*
B: *Okay. Keep in touch!*
A: *You too! Bye!*

*　　*　　*

A: *See you later.*
B: *Okay. Take care of yourself.*
A: *You too. G'bye.*

A: あいつは誰？
B: フィルのことですか？ 彼は私と一緒にダーツをする人です。

*　　*　　*

A: あの女性は誰ですか？
B: 彼女はグレンが付き合ってる娘です。

*　　*　　*

A: あのかわいい顔した背が低い娘は誰ですか？
B: スージーのこと？ 彼女が、僕が君に話していた娘だよ。

*　　*　　*

A: あの女性は何歳ですか？
B: ベティのこと？ 彼女は２０代前半です。

*　　*　　*

A: ビールをありがとう。
B: どういたしまして。

*　　*　　*

A: 今年、教えてくれてありがとう。
B: どういたしまして。

*　　*　　*

A: じゃ、もう行かなきゃ。さよなら。
B: うん。連絡してね。
A: うん。君も。じゃあね。

*　　*　　*

A: じゃあ、またね。
B: うん、身体に気をつけてね。
A: 君もね。じゃあね。

LEARN THESE SENTENCES

1 ...をありがとう。 Thanks for ...

Look at the diagram. Do you understand?

Thanks for reading this!

ポイント	英語	文章
感謝 →	Thanks for ... →	*Thanks for* (名詞) → *the beer.* / *everything.*
		Thanks for (名詞) → *helping.* / *coming.*

Thanks for carrying my books.

	日本語	英語
例 1	食事をありがとう。(ご馳走様でした。) →	*Thanks for the meal.*
例 2	来てくれてありがとう。 →	*Thanks for coming.*
例 3	コンピュータの使い方を教えてくれてありがとう。 →	*Thanks for showing me how to use the computer.*

Speak English everyday!
Thanks for your advice.

2 ...のことですか？ You mean ... ?

Look at the diagram. Do you understand?

標準日本語	標準英語	会話的
...のことですか？ →	Do you mean ... ? →	*You mean ... ?*

You mean "drunk"... ?

	日本語	英語
例 1	シアトル・マリナーズで活躍した日本人の野球選手は誰でしたか？ イチローのことですか？ →	*Who is the Japanese baseball player that played for the Seattle Mariners?* *You mean Ichiro?*
例 2	血を吸う奴ってなんというの？ 吸血鬼のことですか？ →	*What do you call a blood sucker?* *You mean vampire?*
例 3	スパイダーマンの名前はなんだっけ？ あ、ピーター・パーカーのことですか？ →	*What is Spiderman's name?* *Oh, you mean Peter Parker?*

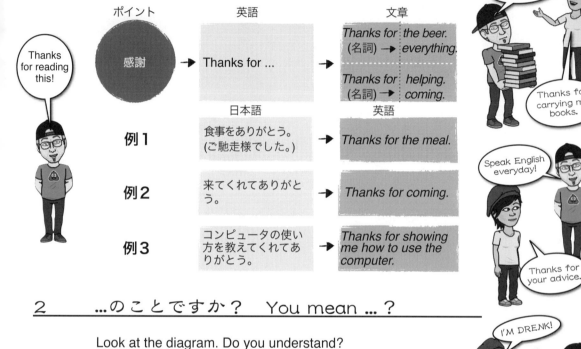

I will fight the man with a black helmet.
You mean Darth Vader?

LEARN THESE SENTENCES

3　　...をしてる男の人です。　　He's the guy that ...

Look at the diagram. Do you understand?

ポイント	文1	文2

関係代名詞 →
Pete is a guy. ／ I play tennis with **him**.

↓ ／ ↓

Pete is a guy　that　I play tennis with.

Pete のことを2回言わなくていいので、 him がなくなる。

Peter is a guy that I play tennis with.

Who is your friend?

He's a guy that I met at the airport.

Can you see the pattern?

例1

Jane is a nice lady. ／ **She** is in my class.

↓ ／ ↓

Jane is a nice lady　that　is in my class.

同じように Jane のことを2回言わなくていいので、 she がなくなる。

Jane is a nice lady that is in my class.

He's the guy that follows me.

例2

Hana is an old woman. ／ I met **her** in Tokyo.

↓ ／ ↓

Hana is an old woman that　I met　in Tokyo.

Hana is an old woman that I met in Tokyo.

Where are we going?

Led Zeppelin concert!

Led Zeppelin is a band that I like.

テキストのストーリー訳は、直訳ではなく自然な訳にした。

ポイント	英 --> 日　直訳	会話的・自然
直訳 vs 意訳	Glen's a guy that I go climbing with.　グレンは私と一緒に登山をする人です。	*Glen's a guy that I go climbing with.*　グレンとは一緒に登山に行ったの
例	Franklin's the guy that teaches me aerobics.　フランクリンは私にエアロビクスを教える人です。	*Franklin's the guy that teaches me aerobics.*　フランクリンは 私にエアロビクスを教えてくれたの。

Who's he?

He's a guy that I do yoga with.

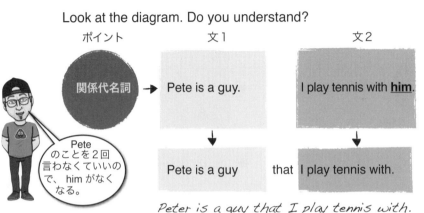

別れ

LEARN THESE SENTENCES

4 　...３０代前半です。　　... in his/her early 30s.

Look at the diagram. Do you understand?

ポイント	日本語	英語
年齢	... 前半	*in his/her early ... s*
	... 半ば	*in his/her mid ... s*
	... 後半	*in his/her late ... s*

	日本語	英語
例1	エリは２０代前半です。	*Eri is in her early 20s.*
例2	ドンは７０代半ばです。	*Don is in his mid 70s.*
例3	ジムは１０代後半です。	*Jim is in his late teens.*

How old is he?

I don't know. Maybe he's in his mid 40s?

電話でも手紙でもEメールでもいいから、とにかく連絡してください、という意味だよ。

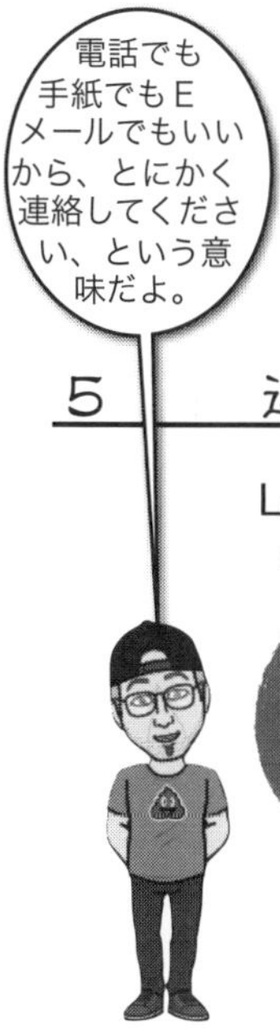

5 　連絡してね。　Keep in touch.

Look at the diagram. Do you understand?

標準日本語	標準英語	会話的
連絡して...	Stay in contact.	*Keep in touch.*

	日本語	英語
	もう行かなくちゃ。連絡してね、さよなら。	*I gotta go. Keep in touch. See ya.*

So, let's keep in touch, OK?

6 　気をつけてね。　Take care.

同じように、別れるときの定番挨拶です。

Look at the diagram. Do you understand?

標準日本語	標準英語	会話的
気をつけてください。	Please take care of yourself.	*Take care!*

	日本語	英語
	またね。気をつけてね。	*See ya later. Take care!*

See ya later guys!

Take care!

CHALLENGE STAGE

Challenge 1. *Fill in the blanks from the list.*

1 George: Hey Dan. This is a really great party. みんなを呼んでくれて、ありがとう。

2 Dan: That's okay, George. We're all going to miss you.

3 George: Well ... 行きたくないけれど、行かなくてはなりません。

4 Dan: Yeah, that's too bad. ところで、知らない人がひとりかふたりいるよ。

5 George: Who don't you know?

6 Dan: Well, who's that guy over there?

7 George: アルのことですか？ He's the guy that I go hiking with.

8 Dan: Oh, I see. あのでっかい耳している人は誰？

9 George: That's Ross. 彼はテキサスで会った人だよ。

10 Dan: We're really going to miss you, George.

11 George: I don't want to leave, but I have to. I'm sorry Dan.

12 Dan: That's okay. ちゃんと連絡してね、ジョージ。

13 George: You keep in touch too. 身体に気を付けてください、ダン。

14 Dan: Okay. Goodbye George.

Choose the best sentence for the blanks:

a) Keep in touch, George.

b) Who's the guy with the big ears?

c) I don't want to go but I have to.

d) By the way, there's 1 or 2 people here that I don't know.

e) And take care of yourself, Dan.

f) You mean Al?

g) Thanks for inviting everyone.

h) He's the guy that I met in Texas.

CHALLENGE STAGE

Challenge 2. *Circle the correct answer.*

1. Which sentence is the same as *Are you talking about Donald?*
   (a) You mean Donald? (b) Are you mean Donald?
   (c) Is Donald mean? (d) Donald is mean?

2. A friend helps you wash your car. What should you say?
   (a) Thanks by washing me. (b) Thanks for helping me.
   (c) Thanks to helping me. (d) Thanks of washing me.

3. On your birthday, your friends give you some beer. What should you say?
   (a) Thanks to the beer. (b) Thanks by the beer.
   (c) Thanks of the beer. (d) Thanks for the beer.

4. Rod is a guy. I go skiing with him. You can say;
   (a) Rod's a guy that go skiing. (b) Rod's a guy that I go skiing.
   (c) Rod's a guy that he go skiing. (d) Rod's a guy that I go skiing with.

5. Kay is a lady. She teaches me yoga. You can say;
   (a) Kay's a lady that I teach yoga. (b) Kay's a lady that she teaches yoga.
   (c) Kay's a lady that yoga teach me. (d) Kay's a lady that teaches me yoga.

6. Queen is a rock band. I like them. You can say;
   (a) Queen is a band that I like. (b) Queen is a band that I like them.
   (c) Queen is a band that like me. (d) Queen is a band that like.

7. If Justin is 25 years old, we can say:
   (a) He is in his early 20s. (b) He is in his mid 20s.
   (c) He is in his late 20s. (d) He is in his average 20s.

8. Only one expression is correct. Which one?
   (a) Bill is in late 70s. (b) Taro is in early 30s.
   (c) Jack is in his 45s. (d) Angie is in her 40s.

9. If you want a friend to write or mail you, you should say:
   (a) Please keep on touch. (b) Please keep in touch.
   (c) Please keep by touch. (d) Please touch me.

10. When we say goodbye to somebody, we often ALSO say:
    (a) You care take. (b) Care taker.
    (c) Take care you. (d) Take care.

14h
別れ

CHALLENGE STAGE

Challenge 3. Did you read the English story?
Let's check!

1. At the beginning, Yoko says to John;
   - *(i) Thanks for inviting everyone.*
   - *(ii) Thanks for inviting me.*
   - *(iii) Thanks for inviting my mother.*
   - *(iv) Thanks for not inviting my mother.*

2. Who does Yoko go mountain-biking with?
   - *(i) She goes mountain-biking with Eric.*
   - *(ii) She goes mountain-biking with Ron.*
   - *(iii) She goes mountain-biking with Brick.*
   - *(iv) She goes mountain-biking with Wendy.*

3. Who is the guy with the backpack?
   - *(i) The guy with the backpack is Glenn.*
   - *(ii) The guy with the backpack is Ron.*
   - *(iii) The guy with the backpack is Brick.*
   - *(iv) The guy with the backpack is Franklin.*

4. Who is the short guy with no hair?
   - *(i) The short guy with no hair is Ron.*
   - *(ii) The short guy with no hair is Glenn.*
   - *(iii) The short guy with no hair is John.*
   - *(iv) The short guy with no hair is Brick.*

5. Who is Franklin?
   - *(i) Franklin is the guy that Yoko works with.*
   - *(ii) Franklin is Yoko's aerobics teacher.*
   - *(iii) Franklin is the guy in the kitchen.*
   - *(iv) Franklin is the guy she met at Al's Bar.*

6. Who is Brick?
   - *(i) Brick is the guy that Yoko works out with.*
   - *(ii) Brick is Yoko's aerobics teacher.*
   - *(iii) Brick is the guy in the kitchen.*
   - *(iv) Brick is the guy she met at Al's Bar.*

7. Who's the lady standing in the kitchen?
   - *(i) The lady in the kitchen is Linda.*
   - *(ii) The lady in the kitchen is Yoko.*
   - *(iii) The lady in the kitchen is Wendy.*
   - *(iv) The lady in the kitchen is Brick.*

8. Where did Yoko meet Wendy?
   - *(i) Yoko met Wendy in Tokyo.*
   - *(ii) Yoko met Wendy at John's party.*
   - *(iii) Yoko met Wendy at Al's Bar.*
   - *(iv) Yoko met Wendy in the gym.*

9. How old is Wendy?
   - *(i) She's in her late 20s.*
   - *(ii) She's in her early 30s.*
   - *(iii) She's in her mid 20s.*
   - *(iv) She's in her late 20s.*

10. John tells Yoko to;
    - *(i) keep in touch and drink beer.*
    - *(ii) drink beer and take care.*
    - *(iii) keep in touch and take care.*
    - *(iv) drink beer and get married.*

著者略歴
Simon Thollar ソーラ･サイモン　1960年7月生まれ

北海道情報大学 経営情報学部 システム情報学科 教授　simon@do-johodai.ac.jp
1982年　タスマニア公立大学 文学士
1983年　タスマニア公立大学 教育学修士
1987年　タスマニア公立大学 特別支援教育修士
2004年　シェフィールド大学（英国）日本文化論修士

主たる研究業績

「SpeakOut!」第2版発行 丸善プラネット株式会社 2003
「Hobbyman」第2版発行 丸善プラネット株式会社 2003
「Does being "globally minded" facilitate English learning in university students?」
韓国英語教育学会（KOTESOL）年次国際大会Proceeding 2018
「Transitions in Faculty Awareness: Exploring What University Students Don't Like About Teachers」
韓国英語教育学会（KOTESOL）年次国際大会Proceedings 2016
「Applying digital game-based language learning to improve /l/ and /r/ phoneme discrimination」
韓国英語教育学会（KOTESOL）年次国際大会Proceedings 2015
「Motivating Students With Humorous One-Point Videos.」
JALT2012 Conference Proceedings. Oct 12-15, 2012, Tokyo: JALT, pp.506-515. 2013
「The Application of Entertaining, One-Point Videos in Remedial English Education」
北海道情報大学紀要論文 第25巻1号,pp.1-14. 2013
「Improving teaching skills and strategies through awareness of individual teaching traits」
北海道情報大学紀要論文 第24巻2号,pp.15-28. 2012
「The design and construction of a readily accessible on-line student skills taxonomy to quantify abilities」
北海道情報大学紀要論文 第24巻1号,pp.17-32. 2012
「Improving auditory L/R discrimination through the design and implementation of serious games」
北海道情報大学紀要論文 第24巻1号,pp.1-15. 2012
など

Simon Says
—Basic English Conversation for Young Adults

2019 年 2 月 28 日　初版発行
2024 年 2 月 28 日　第6刷発行

著 作 者　Simon Thollar　©2019

発 行 所　丸善プラネット株式会社
〒101-0051　東京都千代田区神田神保町二丁目17番
電 話（03）3512-8516
http://planet.maruzen.co.jp/

発 売 所　丸善出版株式会社
〒101-0051　東京都千代田区神田神保町二丁目17番
電 話（03）3512-3256
https://www.maruzen-publishing.co.jp/

組版：株式会社オメガ・コミュニケーションズ
印刷・製本：株式会社留萌新聞社 印刷事業部 あるふぁらんど

ISBN 978-4-86345-418-7　C0082